What Readers are saying...

"Dave Barry does Slovakia could be the subtitle of this book. And P.J. O'Rourke, look out!" - Marjorie Heidorn

*"Read this to learn how to **mime kitty litter in a foreign country**. If you go to Slovakia to learn, maybe you **want to get strip-searched at the border?"*** - Jack Wayman

*"Slovakia. **Who knew?"*** - Bonnie Pattiz

*"I really, really, really enjoyed reading this! I really, really, really wish I could come up with the perfect quote so **everyone will read this book!"*** - Al Herget

*"The humor is buried deep within cynicism, a **perfect combination** to write about the absurd."* - Jan Inscho

"Paints powerful pictures precisely, producing perfect perception. The pick of the literate." - Larry Barfield

*"Being from Western Europe, I didn't expect this book about Eastern Europe to be **droll or enthralling**. Wrong. **Bob's your uncle!"*** - Pauline Lesley Alexandra Richard

*"If you like to giggle, snicker, hoot, snort, cackle, chortle, chuckle, or guffaw, **read this book."*** - Cathy Helton

*"**Laugh or cry, but read it!"*** - Loretta Flipse, M.D.

*"Do you think Dennis Miller is funny but all you understand are the expletives, or do you rely on Rush Limbaugh or Al Franken for your beliefs? If you do, then I highly recommend you **replace this book with something similarly priced you can eat."*** - Danny S. Jones

ABSURDISTAN

ABSURDISTAN

*The lighter side of life
in the Soviet Bloc
after the Evil Empire*

A true story by
R. Lee Wright, Ph.D.

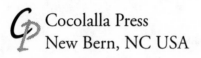
Cocolalla Press
New Bern, NC USA

Absurdistan
Copyright © 2005 by R. Lee Wright
All rights reserved.

Published by
Cocolalla Press
New Bern, NC 28560
www.cocolallapress.com

First Edition 2005

ISBN 0-9760780-9-0

Library of Congress Control Number 2004096688

Cover Artwork and Design by R. Lee Wright

To order a copy of this book, please go to
www.cocolallapress.com

Cataloging-in-Publication
Wright, R. Lee.
    Absurdistan: The Lighter Side of Life in the
Soviet Bloc after the Evil Empire / by R. Lee Wright.

    I. Title

ISBN 0-9760780-9-0 (pbk.)
    1. Travel 2. Humor 3. Soviet Union
    4. Eastern Europe 5. Slovakia

Printed in the United States of America

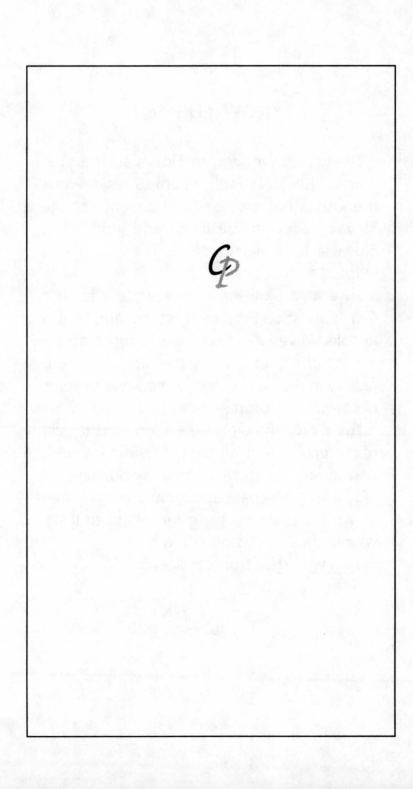

ACKNOWLEDGMENTS

Living and working in Slovakia for a year made writing this book possible. The generous friendship, humor, help, and patience of the Slovak people made living and working in Slovakia for a year possible. Thank you all. I learned a great deal.

I went to Slovakia as a volunteer for the Civic Education Project. This program, begun at Yale University, places western professors in eastern European universities to help faculty and students overcome seventy years of communist propaganda.

I have recounted my experiences to the best of my recollection, armed only with a learner's permit for a poetic license. If my portrayal of Slovakia and Slovaks annoys anyone, feel free to write a book showing me trying to learn your language, customs, and history.

That would be truly comical.

THANKS

To my wife Larysa, and
our children Will and Grace,
who encouraged me
to publish this book.

A special thanks to
Will's Godmother,
Marjorie, who made me
write it in the first place.

An assist goes to
Will's Godfather,
Jack, who provided
key ideas.

A final thanks to
my mother, Jnita,
who encouraged, cajoled,
and edited until my
ramblings became a book.

"Complexity in the mind
is not caused by learning.
Learning is caused by
complexity in the mind."
- Steven Pinker

"The whole point of education is
surely to exercise those brain circuits
that might be needed in life --- rather than to
stuff the mind full of facts."
- Matt Ridley

Table of Contents

Photo Credits

Slovak Words Inside

ano (good)	170
becherovca (local alcohol)	112
bolshoi (big)	174
burciak (first pressing of grapes)	79
dobre (good)	67
dobre den (good day)	20
dom kultury (house of culture)	79
dovidenia (see you later, alligator)	20
jeden (one)	66
krown (1 krown = 30 cents)	19
langose (fried bread)	66
macka (cat)	78
mnozstvo (amount)	33
nie (no)	17
panelak (high rise building)	13
pazalsta (please)	170
petrzalka (high rise suburb)	24
pivo (beer)	67
poleizi (police)	146
politology (political science)	29
potraviny (grocery store)	18
priatelka (girlfriend)	27
restaurace (restaurant)	17
slivovitch (local alcohol)	112
stare mesto (old town)	19
studene (cold)	169
trznica (farmers/flea market)	57
vino (wine)	114
vyjst (go out)	33
zima (winter)	103
zmrzlina (ice cream)	33

"Hasta La Vista, Communista!"

1

The Evil Empire

"Mr. Gorbachov,
tear this wall down."
President Reagan

Baby Volkswagens being born wake me up. Piercing, excruciating, crashing metal persuades me that the stork is dropping the automotive infants from an altitude of 12,000 feet, impacting just outside my window. *These new model storks must have precision-guided bundles,* my wooly brain surmises. *Or maybe storks are extinct; these are cruise bundles, launched from offshore subs.*

Daylight is beginning to skulk in my window in this ex-communist, high-rise apartment building, called a "panelak." A vast cornfield on one side, and an equally vast auto factory on the other bracket this particular panelak; my flat is on the factory side. I am about ten kilometers northwest of Bratislava, the capital of Slovakia. The new Slovak Republic being the newest country, in the new world of Eastern Europe.

Volkswagens must arrive in the world kicking and screaming, the same as any other baby, my sleepy fantasy continues, *except magnitudes louder.* I just learned my first lesson in Eastern Europe: your average Slovakian, unlike me, does not consider 5:30 a.m. all that early to begin the workday.

Long Ago And Far Away

Yesterday I boarded an airplane, to fly thousands of miles around the world. *Why am I going to a city I've never heard of,* I asked myself rhetorically, *in a country that didn't exist a few years ago, much less when I learned geography?* This is a city, in a country, in a region, that has known nothing but communism in my lifetime.

A few days ago, I was minding my own business, your average American university professor. Then I received an invitation to come to Eastern Europe, to help reform universities that had been teaching nothing but communist doctrine for seventy years. As hard as I try, it is impossible for me to think of post-communism except in negative terms, like a hole in the ground is a lack of dirt.

A previous "volunteer" for the infiltration of Eastern European higher education came to her senses, bailing out at the last second. Now they needed a pinch hitter, someone who didn't have time to think before jumping: me. Someone who had barely enough time to grab some books and clothes, cry goodbye to family and friends, and sprint to the airplane.

Would you come, the invitation entreated, *and would you bring your western textbooks and teaching methods? Please come,* the invitation implored, *just now?* An offer I couldn't refuse. Now I am here for a year, a volunteer, to teach graduate courses in a new university. More importantly, I am here to help rebuild higher education in an ancient university, replacing some of the communist propaganda.

An optimist, I trust this is not an oxymoron. Before I left, a colleague warned me that, "working with most ex-communists may be like trying to teach a pig to sing, it accomplishes nothing, it merely annoys the pig."

RUDE AWAKENING

Struggling to focus my eyes, and focus my mind, I stare without comprehension at the tiny, sparsely furnished room. Crash, bang, shriek. *Oh yeah,* I think painfully, *now I remember something about a Volkswagen (Volkswagen?) factory.*

Fragments of memory from last night are dripping back now, slowly, like Chinese water torture. Fighting a losing battle for a few more seconds of sleep, I finally succumb to the "din of iniquity" and get up, rationalizing with the mental cliché "if you snooze you lose."

It takes no more than two seconds to complete a visual inventory of my new home. *That's strange,* I think, *the room is square, not the usual rectangle.* The efficiency apartment is outfitted with a small bed, and a tiny square table with two metal chairs that look like a dinette set right out of a 1957 Sears and Roebuck mail-order catalog. There is a square sink in the corner and a square hot plate on the square counter beside it. *Where is the square refrigerator,* my thought finishes, *there has to be a refrigerator, hasn't there?* Evidently not.

As Andy Kaufman, the well-known sociologist, said in his comedy routines about life in Eastern Europe, "I have everything that is required. I have the table, I have the chair, and I have the bucket."

On the positive side, this panelak is unusual in that there is a small, square balcony for each apartment; mine overlooks the VW factory, which is all I can see from the balcony. Not only can I see it, if I lean out over the railing, I swear I can touch it. I also see a huge pipe (one meter in diameter) running from the factory and disappearing into the Hobbit. Should I worry? Don't ask. I don't know.

I lucked out, I think, *this flat is not too bad, and bigger than I expected.*

The lack of a refrigerator is, as we say here, a "beeg" problem. When I say "beeg," I am not making fun of the way people talk in Slovakia, or anywhere else. It is just that "i" in the Slovak language is pronounced as "e" in English, and has a long sound like the word 'feet,' so the word "big" comes out sounding something like "beeeeg." Since almost every statement here begins "we have a beeg problem," no matter what comes next, this phrase quickly comes to be an eastern European mantra.

POLITICS MAKES STRANGE BEDFELLOWS

One of the more conspicuous failures of modern social science was the spectacular inability of political science and or sociology to correctly predict the occurrence, much less the unbelievable speed, of the collapse of communism. With the benefit of "50-50" hindsight, we can easily see that Karl Marx was right in making all of those dire predictions. Marx envisioned a government exploiting the worker, ultimately withering away.

What communism manifestly (sorry, I couldn't resist) couldn't comprehend, and what we didn't discern, was that the government that Marx imagined was communism, not capitalism. He had everything backwards, and once the communist states started withering, they withered at the speed of light.

Dialing Karl's cell phone (he has an unlisted number), I ask, "how did you manage to screw up so badly? People are starting to think that you are an idiot."

He protests, "Hey, I really meant communism all the time! It was a simple translation error: capitalism, communism; they both start with a C. Sue me."

Even Slovakian kids laugh at me,
when they see I live
in the panelak I call the "Hobbit."

With that remark, Marx demonstrates he has learned the main lesson of capitalism: sue someone. As Pogo sagely observed, "We have met the enemy, and he is us." This is what happens when you confuse freedom with license.

Up The Down Staircase

Later, I found a refrigerator that was available in a vacant room on a different floor, but there was no one to move it. I borrowed the key to that room and, fortunately for me, it was small and light enough (as all refrigerators here are) for one person to pick up and carry. That solved the first beeg problem of life in Eastern Europe

I get dressed and walk down three flights of stairs. Here, the ground floor is number 0. The next floor up is number 1, the next floor number 2, and so on. If there is a basement, this is -1. *Is that why*, I wonder, *we call a place ground zero?* This makes entirely too much sense, so it is difficult for me to comprehend. In many buildings, the ground floor is two stories tall with commensurate high ceilings, so to get to the second floor requires three flights of stairs. Later, I roll the dice once, riding the communist elevator. That tiny, rusted, self-service box is too noisy and scary, so I make the stairs a way of life in Eastern Europe.

When I get to floor 0, the ground floor, I am suddenly hungry. I decide to ask about breakfast possibilities. Since the Slovakian word for restaurant is "restaurace," I think this will be a piece of cake. *Maybe not,* the thought continues under its own power, *I don't even know the word for cake in Slovak.*

A bored young woman is trying unsuccessfully to hide behind the undersized front desk. She never takes her eyes off what appears to be a Mexican soap opera on a small, fuzzy, black and white TV set. Approaching the desk, I dig the Slovak/English dictionary out of my backpack.

Bravely, after only one lesson in survival Slovak, I attempt to say "Pardon me, is there a 'restaurace' here?"

After a couple of tries with different pronunciation, the one word response comes back, "nie" (no).

I know exactly what that means, I think, mixing my languages, *no way, José. Oh yeah,* I think, *I forgot I am out here in the cornfield by the VW factory.* Changing the subject, I try again, "is there is a potraviny (grocery store) here?"

"Nie, nie," barks the double-barreled answer, blowing away my first attempt at conversation in Slovakian.

A Home Away From Home

Due to the current (and probably permanent) housing shortage in Bratislava, the university that invited me to come here is using this panelak as a convenient source of faculty housing. Most current residents, however, are laborers who cannot find or afford housing in town. Many are from even poorer countries than Slovakia.

Westerners, rich by local standards, push up the price of housing to the point where impoverished local residents get railroaded (or bused, in this case) out of town. This has become a huge dorm for transients and other homeless people; like me. After the "velvet revolution" in 1989, I guess they could not make even the factory workers live here any longer.

What happens is that when a westerner comes to town, they ask the first person they meet who speaks English, "what is the going rent?" Someone will immediately ask, "can you pay in hard currency, preferably Deutschmarks or (the second choice) U.S. dollars?"

"Sure, why not?" you answer.

"Well then," comes the reply, "my cousin happens to have a two bedroom flat, completely furnished with phone and satellite TV, for only $250.00 a month."

"Great," you almost shout, "I'll take it, is ten minutes too soon?" All the while thinking, *this is a steal.*

What you don't know is that the cousin couldn't rent it for half that to a local resident. He takes your $250.00, puts it in a hard currency bank account that pays actual interest, and finds another place to live, temporarily, for 4500 Slovak krowns (about $150.00). This pushes someone below him, who can't even come up with the 4500 krowns, out into the street; maybe eventually all the way out to the Hobbit with me. This is what happens when you confuse America with the rest of the world.

Breakfast Rerun

Changing tactics, I decide to take the bus to the "Stare Mesto" (Old Town) sector of Bratislava. Surely, I can find something for breakfast there. Gamely interrupting the soap opera yet again, I venture another question: "do you have a bus schedule?" adding hand signals and appropriate sound effects, as I am linguistically challenged.

"Ola," the Mexican soap opera on TV blurts out, ¿"coma esta usted"?

The girl glances at me while aiming and firing a disgusted look in Esperanto. I have no trouble understanding that language. Without deigning to answer, she takes the time to dig a schedule out, using Braille, from under the papers scattered on the desk. All the while keeping her eyes and ears glued on the screen. I feel like an idiot, but it works. Pay dirt.

I have made my first successful solo communication in the Slovak language. Proudly accepting the rumpled photocopy of the schedule handed to me, I squint to read it. I squint harder; what is wrong with this picture? Finally it dawns on me, although it is for the correct bus, it is for the wrong bus stop. The times given have no relevance to THIS location. Don't ask. I don't know.

Since only a single bus ventures all the way out to the Hobbit, I decide that the schedule is irrelevant, I will just catch the next bus that comes along, and not one I missed while interrupting the soap opera. Saying "dovidenia" (see you later, alligator) to the girl who is permanently absorbed by the soap, I head out to the bus stop.

Opening the front door, (the only way out of this monolith I later discover) I notice a sign: "HoByt" which I have been mispronouncing as "Hobbit." I glance up at the towering panelak, just thankful that I am not required to live next-door IN the VW factory.

Verification for my theory arrives in the form of a bus, which shows up a mere 21 minutes after I get to the bus stop. Riding the nearly empty bus to the outskirts of Bratislava, I transfer to a trolley for the balance of the trip. Here we have electric buses, autobuses, trolleys, and trams: I usually call them all buses. This two-bus shuffle instantly becomes a way of life for the duration.

Something Old, Something New

When I finally arrive in Stare Mesto, I start looking for something to eat related to breakfast in the USA. I don't bother trying to track down an IHOP or Denny's. I want to experience a real Slovak restaurant, even if I know nothing about Slovakian food.

Several sidewalk cafes spill out into the middle of the street, and I cruise by slowly, peering deep into plates of food. I'm trying to divine the identity of something before I commit myself. The restaurant patrons regard my aberrant behavior suspiciously, correctly.

"Dobre den, Doctor Wright," intrudes a voice from just behind my right elbow. I recognize "dobre den" (good day) but who could possibly recognize me? By an amazing coincidence (or maybe not?) I have managed to run into the only person I have actually met in Bratislava, Ludmilla.

Ludmilla is to be my 'minder' at one of the universities where I will teach. She was the one who met me at the bus from Prague late yesterday, and dropped me off like a night deposit out at the Hobbit.

"Uh, good morning," I reply, "I was, uh, just, uh, trying to find something to, uh, eat."

"You do not know what to eat?" she said.

"Uh, not really," I offer lamely. I should add that Ludmilla's English is probably the best at the university.

"Not a beeg problem. I will teach YOU, yes?" Ludmilla said, favoring me with her Mona Lisa impression.

WALLY WORLD

"Ludmilla," I ask, "what's the story on that castle across the street?" taking the opportunity to get a free history lesson by pumping her for information during breakfast

"Oh, Bratislava Castle," she nods in the direction of a huge stone wall curving in both directions, "I'll tell you about that sometime, after you study our history for a while." That was Ludmilla, subtlety and persistently reminding the teacher of his ignorance.

Later, I learn that Bratislava was originally a walled city at the foot of Bratislava Castle, hard by the Danube River (I don't know what "hard by" means, exactly, but I have always wanted to say it). Most of the towering wall that originally surrounded and protected the city is gone. There is only one gate, Michael's Gate, left standing out of the original magnificent seven. Many of the initial buildings, remarkably, are still in place, and about one third of these are under reconstruction since the revolution in 1989, including the remaining wall section and gate.

Since we are sitting at a table out in the middle of the street, I can clearly see the balcony on the third floor (I know, here it is actually the second floor), with laundry drying on the rail. "Ludmilla," I ask, pointing to the

Looking north across the Danube, you see the
Bratislava Castle on the hill, also known as the
"upside down four-poster bed."

brightly colored shirts, "What kind of business is on the third floor? Is that a Chinese laundry?"

"Here in Bratislava," Ludmilla patiently explains, "there is life everywhere: shops on the first floor, offices on the second, apartments on the rest of the floors as well as behind, below, and between everything else."

"You mean people live, love, work, play, drink, have babies, die, do everything right here, in the middle of downtown Old Town?" I ask.

"Precisely," she said, "we don't divide our lives into boxes like you do." Later, Ludmilla said proudly, "I visited America for a week." People here consider her the local USA expert. "Zoning boards in America should start their education here," I mutter.

Ludmilla looks at me quizzically, but doesn't say anything. Some months later, I realize that Slovaks don't have the same curiosity gene that most Americans have. Growing up in a country where asking questions is hazardous to your health exacts a heavy toll.

WAFTING AROUND

After a leisurely breakfast, Ludmilla volunteers to be my guide for the day. *Hmm,* I muse to myself, *is she just taking pity on an ignorant American, or does she secretly work for the secret police?* I dismiss the thought as rookie paranoia, but then I remember the CIA motto: *it's not paranoia if they are really after you.*

Wandering around Stare Mesto with Ludmilla, I discover a charming town, human in scale, used by ordinary citizens and not "run over" by tourists. There are tourists, of course, but they are merely background noise to the hustle and bustle of everyday life. Tourists here don't dominate every photo op. To think that Eastern Europe used to be like the North Pole: everyone knew it was there, but no one visited.

This is Eastern Europe, so the hustle and bustle of everyday life is more like a Vienna waltz, as civilized life should be everywhere. People are welcome to sit in a café with a cup of coffee and a couple of friends all day. No $200.00 an hour consultant has told them, yet, "you can't run a restaurant unless you turn over the customers three times per hour." You gotta love a country that takes the time to observe the amenities of life.

Ancient Rhythms

"Would you like to see my favorite building in Stare Mesto?" Ludmilla asks, snapping me out of my daydream.

"You bet," I reply, failing to consider that she probably doesn't know that particular colloquialism. "Raise your eyes," she said, "you are standing right in front of it."

Looking up, I see a magnificent building in continuous use as a pharmacy since the middle of the fifteenth century. *Wow*, I think, *I'm speechless*. I kick myself for an inadequate (just kidding, nonexistent) architectural education. Even in my ignorance, the detail lovingly crafted into every corner of the building astounds me. Finally, I manage a silent prayer: *Lord, please give the people the will to save and protect this priceless treasure.*

My ignorance of history, the Slovak language, and architecture are running neck and neck and neck, but even I can see that I am not in Kansas anymore.

Outside of Old Town, it's another story. As part of the communist drive to industrialize what had been an agrarian culture, the Soviets developed a gargantuan new town across the Danube River. The entrance to this vast socialistic development is across the Most SNP (the bridge of the Slovak National Uprising). This is the bridge called the "Darth Vader" bridge because of the eerie extraterrestrial flying saucer perched on top. During

Bratislava 's version of a sidewalk cafe.
Put it in the middle of the street,
and park the cars on the sidewalk.

construction, the Soviets brought in bulldozers and simply leveled the Jewish quarter of Old Town.

Later, I will see the movie *Schindler's List* here in Old Town, a few steps from where the Jewish Ghetto used to be. The effect of this movie, seen in Eastern Europe where the events took place, is no doubt the same when seen elsewhere. I also doubt if the effect is any different seeing it in a theater right next to the bridge and freeway, built on the remains of the Jewish Quarter, including synagogues and cemeteries. After all, the Soviets did the bulldozing. I also don't know if it is different sitting in an audience of Slovaks, whose immediate ancestors may (or may not) have participated in similar events.

I do know that it made a difference being so close to the war that was out of control in the former Yugoslavia. My proximity to Bosnia-Herzegovina seems to heighten my awareness of ethnic cleansing and racism of all persuasions. As bad as the war in Bosnia seemed back in the States, it seemed ten times more real here. Here, where my next-door neighbors are a family of Croatian refugees, who seem to get along fine with the Serbs down the hall, and both ignore Muslims walking down the street.

BRIDGE OVER TROUBLED WATER

The bridge built after bulldozing the Jewish quarter connects the new bedroom suburb called "Petrzalka," on the south side of the Danube, with the rest of Bratislava. I think, *maybe this is similar to what happened after the conjoining of Buda and Pest downstream in Hungary.*

The thought of the twins Buda and Pest brings to mind the fascinating case study that is going on between identical twins separated at birth and raised by different parents with extraordinarily different philosophies.

East Germany is, hands down, the luckiest of the former Soviet Satellite states. If only every country had a really rich relative ready. Just think, North Korea could be reclaimed by South Korea, China could be rescued by Hong Kong, and North America could be redeemed by South America, no, wait…well, you get the idea.

Before a wild and crazy government could go off on some harebrained political scheme, it would be required to split the country in half, as a sort of control, like a science experiment in high school. Therefore, if (read when) it all goes badly, the good twin would be waiting, to remerge with the evil twin.

Petrzalka is a gigantic forest of gigantic panelaks notable by being ten and twelve stories tall, as compared to the six to eight stories of mortal panelaks. Clearly a colossus of collectivism. This is what happens when you confuse the economies of scale with the human scale.

The rest of the day, I surf along on Ludmilla's wake, as if she were a tugboat guiding me into harbor. I struggle to keep up while navigating through the sights, sounds, and smells of Old Town.

Occasionally, when the wind is just right, I catch a whiff of sewage from the woefully ancient and inadequate sewerage system in Old Town. *That's O.K.,* I assure myself, *because what I am inhaling is really old, at least a couple of centuries or more, and therefore worth smelling.*

Petrzalka notwithstanding, Old Town has a charm for which developers in America would kill. You gotta love a place where they could film the next Robin Hood movie without changing a thing.

The people walking around Bratislava look a lot like me. Or me like them. Those who appear to be twenty something all wear blue jeans and designer T-shirts, Adidas warm-ups and Nike running shoes, baseball caps with the logos of American professional sports teams and carry a Sony Walkman. You could be in New York, since everyone seems to be speaking a foreign language.

After a long day of tourist travails, I thank Ludmilla profusely. I decide to try to figure out more of the transit system and, simultaneously, determine how to get back to the Hobbit. First, I make a couple of false starts on buses going the wrong direction. In my defense, I might point out that streets in Bratislava, unlike the typical American city, do not run to the points of the compass. They twist, and turn back on themselves, like the plot in an Agatha Christie novel. You board a bus that is heading east, only to have it make an immediate U-turn, and head the opposite way. Don't ask, I don't know.

After inadvertently seeing more of the city than I needed the first day, I finally make it out to the edge of Bratislava. Here I begin the soon-to-be common vigil of "waiting for the night bus" to the VW factory.

During the day, regular buses run every thirty minutes from the city limits out to the Hobbit. After nine o'clock, this drops to one every hour or two, on weekends much less. Living in Eastern Europe is a lot like being in the army, with hurry up and wait being the order of the day.

STRANGER IN A STRANGE LAND

At the last bus stop before leaving town, I am waiting with only one other person, an unusual situation. This guy is wearing an army uniform, which makes sense, since there is an army base even farther out in the cornfield than the Hobbit. This is the first fellow I have seen in uniform, except for the soldiers strolling around Old Town cradling submachine guns.

This soldier doesn't seem to be armed, however I still try to avoid eye contact. "Do you have a match?" he asks in Slovakian, which of course I don't understand yet.

Here is my automatic answer when I don't understand the question: "I'm sorry I speak English." I can't decide exactly how I mean this, but that is how it comes out.

A lively pantomime discussion ensues, which consists of me looking up a word in my English-Slovak dictionary. Then I show him the Slovak translation. He in turn looks up a Slovak word, and shows me the English translation. It turns out that he is a sergeant in what is now the Slovak Army (before the split it was the Czechoslovakian Army), specializing in rockets.

"My father military." I show him the words I say.

"Rank?" he points out with a quizzical expression.

"Colonel." I display.

"Ah, general?" He said this phrase out loud and pronounced it the same as in English, except with a hard 'g,' like 'girl'.

"Nie," I answer. With hand motions, I demonstrate how a colonel is below a general.

"Captain?" He finds and points out the word.

"Colonel." I find the words easily this time, and with more hand motions, show how a colonel is sandwiched between a captain and a general.

"Major?" He tries the inevitable last possibility.

Here we go again. This takes a lot longer to do than to explain, but the bus is late so we have the time. After we finally straighten everything out, I point to him, and then out past the Hobbit. "You...go...army?"

"Nie, nie" he said a big grin. He grabs the dictionary eagerly and looks up a new word, while saying "priatelka, priatelka."

I shake my head, not understanding. Holding out the dictionary one last time, he proudly shows me the word for the exceedingly difficult and dangerous military mission he is on that night: girlfriend! You gotta love a country where this is what they mean by army maneuvers.

2

First Day Of School

"Education is a progressive discovery
of our own ignorance."
Will Durant

Remember when you were six years old? You faced going to school for the first time, the first day. You felt all alone, you didn't understand the big words you just knew people were going to throw at you, and you didn't know anybody. You were terrified; you wanted to hide under the bed. Your imagination went into overdrive creating images of unspeakable humiliation and horror.

My first day at school here was nothing like that, I think, on my way to my new university, via the obligatory two-bus shuffle. First, I decide to write down the bus schedule to avoid excessive, excessive waits. The buses in Bratislava proper are usually either close enough to being on time that it is worth checking the schedule, or they come often enough that it doesn't matter. This is not a law, however. There is no refund.

One university where I will be teaching is the largest institution of higher education in Slovakia. It's an immense place, spread all over Bratislava, in the most unexpected buildings. You can find one classroom here, and another classroom across town. This is not a traditional American campus: i.e. Disneyland for eighteen year olds.

Let's call it Slovak U. Here I will be offering a series of lectures in public policy analysis in the old department of "Politology," which is the Slovak version of Political Science, plus a little history and some economics. Back in the old days in America, before we got so smart, political science was actually called "political economics." Since the days of Bill "it's the economy, stupid" Clinton, we should reinstate the original name and meaning. Of all the courses that the communists would not let be taught, my guess is that policy analysis was right at the top of the list.

A Thought For An Idea

Do you remember that famous communist policy wonk, Henry Kissingerisky, inching into Stalin's office deep under the Kremlin? "

"Comrade Stalin," he begins gingerly, "have you seen this new directive about plowing our potato fields only from west to east and not from east to west?"

"Have I seen it?" Stalin said, "I wrote it, you idiotsky."

"Oh, it is brilliant, of course, and not a word should be changed. I was only thinking," Kissingerisky hesitantly concluded, "we might possibly consider the consequences of having all our tractors at the east end of the field with no way to get them back to the west end? Is it possible, if we don't want our tractors plowing to the west, to consider just plowing only north and south? That way we wouldn't ever need to go to the west."

What? You never heard of Henry Kissingerisky? Exactly. I rest my case.

When someone asks me if I am kidding about stuff like this, I tell them the story of Lysenko. Lysenko was a poor farmer, who through a series of comedy and errors became the most powerful man in communist agriculture. Before being discredited and removed, he had opponents tortured and executed just to cover up crop failures. Millions of people suffered due to the ignorance of this charlatan. This story is a textbook case of politics, stupidity, and greed. Looking for a lesson in this sorry tale, I realize that every country has a Lysenko or two in their closet. This is what happens when you mistake a thought for an idea.

When I arrive at the university, I stop in at the department office of Politology to butter up the department secretary, and learn which faculty and staff to avoid. Slovak U has lots of teachers, quite a few students, and some staff. It has, however, virtually no useful technology like computers, fax machines, photocopiers, and up-to-date books. They do still have all of the stuff the communists left, when they disappeared in the middle of the night, like textbooks by Lysenko. Still, it is better here than in many other countries of Eastern Europe.

Some faculty members prefer the communist era, when money and support were available. The more reform minded faculty value the intellectual freedom. As Lenin never tired of reminding everyone, "freedom is good, control is better."

The department secretary, Svetlana, opens the door after my tentative knock. Unlike their counter-parts in American universities, doors here are always closed, and there are no windows. You just have to roll the dice, and see if there is anybody in, and if they are, will they open the door?

"Hello," I begin, "my name is..."

"Dr. Wright," Svetlana finishes, "please come in."

Whoa, I wonder, *did I land on the set of the Cheers TV show, where everybody knows your name?*

"Oh...oh," I said, "I am sorry to bother you but..."

"Not at all, not at all" Svetlana said, "Ludmilla told us to expect you."

"Thank you, thank you very much," I said, doing my best unintentional Elvis impression, "I was wondering if the director was available for a moment?"

The director of the political science department is, by all accounts, a dynamic and charismatic person. By the force of his personality, he has held this department together through times that would have destroyed a lesser man. He has been a shining light during the dark years of communist control, and he has kept the department provisioned during the last few years of democratic starving.

He is also gone. Unbeknownst to me, he has chosen to take this year off, some kind of ex-communist sabbatical. No doubt, he deserves a vacation, and this would not be a serious problem, except that many of the best students in the department have followed his lead. They are also taking the year off.

We should try this in American universities; give the kids a year off now and then. They slave over hot books all day and night, they stuff their brains full of facts and theories, they keep their noses to the grindstone, they work like dogs to take advantage of the wonderful possibilities of a university education. Nah, just kidding.

The best students here, of course, are the ones who have also made the most progress in learning English, and therefore the ones I had counted on the most, not only to take my classes (given only in English), but also to help the brave students whose English is not so good but who take the classes anyway.

The Darth Vader bridge keeps one eye on
you as you try to escape from Petrzalka.
Hint: don't look up as you go under.

"I am so sorry," Svetlana said, "I understood you had been informed that the director will not be here this year. He is taking, how do you say, a rest?" Later, I found out that the rest is directly related to the budget.

Subsequent to the velvet revolution (and the reduction in state money for higher education), when the university is low on money various faculty and staff are selected to volunteer for a long, unpaid, holiday. How do they survive? When do they return? Why do they return? Have they lost a lot of weight? Don't ask. I don't know.

OFF COURSE

Here at Slovak U, I find I will be sharing a small office with three faculty members. After the revolution, state financial support for universities dropped precipitously, while university support for communist teachings dropped simultaneously. Due to the lack of funding, most of the more able professors left for more lucrative private sector jobs (so they could buy food). Those remaining must hold at least two other jobs in addition to their teaching responsibilities just to make barely enough to survive.

Never mind that now. I decide to see when my courses will be offered, and how many students have signed up. You know that "deer in the headlights" look that people get when you say something that makes absolutely no sense. It was as if I had just dropped in unannounced from the University of Mars and asked a question in Venusian, about the schedule of classes at the University of Pluto. Nothing. Nada. Zero.

Thinking that I had spoken too fast or used unfamiliar words, I tried again, many times and many ways. When we finally agree that we understand each word, I work on the meaning. You have surely heard that sarcastic put down that people use that goes "which part of the word '*no*' don't you understand?" Well, after breaking down my question into single words, and analyzing each one, the answer was simple. Here at Slovak U, they don't have a class schedule, and they don't pre-register students. Simpler than American colleges, like I said.

The procedure is this: you put up some notices around the university about the classes you want to teach, you go to the assigned classrooms at the appointed day and time, and you see if anyone shows up. You gotta love a country where things are so simple.

BUY A VOWEL

I need another lesson in Survival Slovak. I badger one of my new colleagues for some help with my new language. After two hours of "vyjst" (go out), "zmrzlina" (ice cream), and "mnozstvo" (amount), I am ready for the first flight back to the States. O.K., at least I am desperate enough to buy a vowel. I wonder if it is this difficult for someone who speaks a Slavic language to learn English. I recall a bit of doggerel about learning English:

Sally Salter, she was a teacher, who taught,
Her friend, Charlie, was a preacher who praught;
His enemies called him a screecher, who scraught.
His heart, as he saw her, kept sinking, and sunk;
His eye, meeting hers, began winking, and wunk;
While she in her turn, fell to thinking, and thunk.
In secret he wanted to speak, and he spoke,
To seek with his lips what his heart long had soke,
So he managed to let the truth leak, and it loke.
The kiss he was dying to steal, then he stole;
At her feet he wanted to kneel, then he knole;
And he said, I feel better than ever I fole.

It is no wonder that everyone in Eastern Europe is trying to learn English; nothing could be simpler.

While meeting my new colleagues, I noticed each one has a slightly different title. During the coming year I will try, on several occasions, to understand the European system of academic degrees and titles, totally without success. There are apparently several different Ph.D. type degrees, but the title of professor is not automatically bestowed on someone with a Ph.D. who teaches in a university. There are other, unknown, hoops required. Don't ask, I don't know.

Trading Places

Like a baby bird that fell prematurely out of the nest and must learn to fly on the way to the ground, the new country of Slovakia fell into the world in 1993. Another victim of nationalistic fervor. The Slovak Republic simply materialized, seemingly out of thin air. It is so young the labor pains have not yet stopped.

This reverse disappearing act occurred almost simultaneously with the disintegration of one of the former Soviet Bloc countries that resulted from the patching together of World War I rubble. You have to wonder when WE will learn that WE can't create new countries by redrawing maps and lumping individuals together, the way we concoct NFL teams. Maybe if the pay scales were comparable?

A thousand years have elapsed since this region was last an independent country. It has belonged to almost everyone since then, including the Hapsburgs, the Germans, the Hungarians, the Austrians, and finally the communists (now the ex-communists). The Hungarians, who were themselves getting intense pressure from the south, moved their whole capital to Bratislava for a time (just a few hundred years, no big deal). Most rulers, who ruled and then got kicked out, managed a comeback. Not unlike Rocky I, Rocky II, Rocky III ad nauseum.

One of my new colleagues asks, "Do you know what it is like to live in Eastern Europe, stuck between the West and Russia?"

"No," I said, "I can't imagine."

"Did you hear about comrade stretched on chairs with feet in refrigerator and head in oven?" he continues.

"I don't think so," I said.

"When asked how he feeling," my colleague finishes, "the man admits, on average, he pretty comfortable." Somewhat surprisingly, Slovakia was created comfortably, during a curtain call of the Velvet Revolution.

The recent birth of other countries, under analogous circumstances, has been as violent as this one was velvet. Velvet revolution or not, the latest election returns in this newborn republic indicate that Slovakia may make an abrupt swerve to the left: a menacing shift backwards after a promising beginning.

There was no vote when the Slovak Republic declared its independence; the current leader simply announced the fact. In a brand new country, a country sans political history, who can tell what this means? Later, this same guy would form a new government with the leftover communists.

As Nikita Khrushchev famously observed, "politicians are the same all over. They promise to build bridges, even where there are no rivers."

U Brat

In addition to Slovak U, I will be working with a new institution of graduate education in Slovakia, established in 1990 to offer the kinds of programs that were impossible under the communist regime. I learn there were many things that were impossible under the communist regime. I will call this place the University of Bratislava. Later, I will shorten it to the more appropriate, U Brat.

U Brat started with a one-year masters degree in Environmental Management, a two-year program in Public Admin, and a one-year program in Architectural and Cultural Conservation. Plus some economics, I always forget about the economists, I wonder why? Maybe the old joke is true, if you laid all the economists in the world end to end, they still wouldn't reach a conclusion.

U Brat, housed in a new Western style building, is out in the suburbs of Bratislava. It would fit right in any city in America. The local IBM franchise occupies the top two floors, if that tells you anything. Later, the Minister of Culture will drop by to see the operation. After a quick tour, he decides that he wants the building. U Brat moved out the next day.

U Brat is a small institution, with maybe 100 students scattered through the four graduate programs. However here, interestingly, there is also no class registration. Since it is so small, every student takes ALL the classes offered in their chosen program, they have no choice. Yet another interesting facet of this innovative institution is that there is virtually no permanent faculty. Or maybe I should say that the entire faculty is virtual faculty. It works kind of like the opposite of getting students over at Slovak U. Here at U Brat, they have students lined up ready to go, but no faculty.

The administration arranges for a visiting lecturer from a western country, to come and give a two or three day seminar. There is a constant parade of these seminars. Virtually one hundred per cent of the learning experiences of the students are through virtual faculty. It turns out I will be virtually the only faculty member to virtually, I mean actually, live here in Slovakia. This is what happens when you confuse education with learning.

What an interesting concept, students with no faculty. I try to imagine what American universities would be like

The Slovak version of a climbing wall.
Practice here before you head up to the
High Tatras, but watch out for the Gargoyles.

if they were run virtually. Maybe with computer networks, teleconferencing, and the budget squeeze, long distance learning is virtually the future of higher education in America. We could offer virtual degrees for virtual educations. Maybe none of us will have to go to work; we can all have virtual jobs. I wonder what we can all buy with virtual money. Virtually everything?

Unlike Slovak U, U Brat has lots of computers all networked togethe, along with huge photocopiers, fax machines, even a scanner or two. Impressive technology, even for some American universities. The library, however, leaves something to be desired. One tiny room with a few books, and two journals. I check out my office, a big private affair with a window and lots of furniture, all for me. Unlike other universities in Eastern Europe, space and western technology are not a beeg problem at U Brat.

The director of U Brat is a pleasant looking, soft spoken, middle-aged woman, Dr. Vodicova. She has a reputation for being a world-class fundraiser. This means that she can really rake in the grants, Eastern Europe being a hot spot for grants right now. Since U Brat is not accredited by Slovakia, and therefore not eligible for state money, this explains her presence.

The head assistant is a young woman named Stasci, not to be confused with the East German Secret Police called Stasi, although some people warn me that the similarities do not end with the name. Later, I will experience firsthand the penchant for control that Stasci holds the patent on in Slovakia. There also seem to be about two staff for each student: grants are wonderful.

Since there is so much western technology available here at U Brat, I try to begin the process of getting the usual western accouterments; a phone in my office, an email account, a key to the copier room, a teaching assistant (O.K., I'm kidding about the teaching assistant).

THEORY OF RELATIVES

After spending most of the day with no results, I finally give up, and walk down to the bus stop. I am taking the bus down to Old Town to meet some other American professors for dinner. It turns out that there are quite a few Americans from various organizations teaching here

The organization I represent here, attached to Yale University, brings over more than one hundred professors from the USA, and spreads them over fifteen countries. The Fulbright scholarship organization ships over a boatload every year, and many other organizations get in the game, as well.

It's a funny thing, but I have a real knack for just missing the bus here in Slovakia. I wrote down the schedules so that I could avoid waving wistfully as the bus pulls away without me, but it always seems that if I get to the bus stop one second late, the bus was early. If I get there early, the bus is invariably late. I am always waiting.

It should average out, but "noooo." The law of averages has been repealed in ex-communist countries. Not being able to figure out this problem in applied physics, I call Albert Einstein up on his cell phone and say, "how come I always miss the bus here in Eastern Europe?"

"You know, I always had the same problem in Berlin," Einstein said, "I missed every bus. It reminds me of the one other problem that I never solved," Einstein said, warming up to the topic, "you know that in a pair of electrons, one always spins one way and the other spins the opposite way?"

I don't, but I said "yeah, sure" so he will hurry up and finish the story.

"Vell," Einstein continues, "if you grab one electron and stick it in one of those leak proof baggies, seal it up, and take it all the way around to the other side of the world, leaving the other one behind, what happens?"

Here I am, running after a bus
I just missed in Slovakia.

"You tell me," I mutter cagily, expecting a trick question.

"Vell," Einstein said, "if you can reverse the spin of the electron that you have with you on the other side of the world, the other electron that you left behind reverses its spin at EXACTLY the same time. How does it know?"

It is a trick question, so I play dumb, grunting "huh?"

Einstein ignores my outburst and goes on, "hey, I guess everything is relative, good luck catching the bus, I never could figure it out."

Sounds Fishy

I find my new colleagues at the designated restaurant with no trouble. Since this is my first real meal in Slovakia, I order the best thing on the menu, trout (this menu being also in German, trout is the only thing I recognize). The trout is good, but the bill is higher than expected.

On closer inspection of the menu, it turns out that trout goes by the gram. There is a base charge and then so much for every gram of fish. Actually, every menu has the weight of the food next to the item, so that you know if you are getting 370 grams of spaghetti, or 150 grams of soup. Even the drinks show you how many deciliters of Pepsi™ or beer will arrive. Here is a tip for you would be tourists in Eastern Europe: when you order bottled water, make sure the bottle is still sealed when it arrives at the table. If not, you will drink tap water of dubious origin.

As always, some places carry these extra charges too far, I later found out. When I got the bill in a Chinese restaurant, and checked the itemized bill, I found out that I had paid a hefty surcharge for the condiments, the chopsticks, and even the napkins. It turns out that, opposite to the American experience, Chinese restaurants are the most expensive places to eat in Bratislava. Don't ask, I don't know.

POLITICS MAKES STRANGE BEDFELLOWS

We are in the middle of the Slovak national political campaigns, so the next day at lunchtime I head over to a political rally in the park, to see the new democracy in action. There are folk dancers dancing in folk costumes, native singers singing native songs in native outfits, and kids passing out campaign buttons and campaign literature. There is also a melodious soothing preamble by a smooth inspirational speaker who would be right at home as the minister in a Southern Baptist Church.

There are sack races, coin tosses, and Frisbees™, everything but the politician. There are kids, dogs, and balloons: the whole catastrophe. The folk band keeps playing the same tune over and over until finally the woman who is the candidate appears. She does not give a speech.

Instead, the Southern Baptist Minister glides through the audience trying to find a volunteer to ask a question after getting a microphone shoved into her face. Failing to get someone to play along, he resorts to asking his own pet questions. Amazingly enough, the candidate has an answer for these.

Since I don't understand the questions or the answers, I play Frisbee with a boy and his dog. Dogs are everywhere in Slovakia, even in the middle of political rallies. There are also a few cats, but you rarely see them. Cats, considered just one small evolutionary step above a rat, live outside almost wild.

DOGGONE

As Slovakia is confirmed dog country, I will take this opportunity to relate a couple of other dog stories. While riding the bus one day, I watch a young girl speak lovingly to the young puppy she carries in her arms. Dogs are allowed on buses and trams as long as they have a muzzle, but even this requirement is ignored on occasion. I realize, while this tender interlude unfolds, that the puppy understands more Slovak words than I do. I redouble my efforts to improve my vocabulary, feeling that my level of comprehension should stay ahead of the puppy.

A new Slovak friend lives in an old apartment in an old neighborhood with some young families, but also some elderly people who have lived in the same place forever. Across the street are some reconstructed luxury apartments filled with well off foreign diplomats (who get paid in hard currency). These diplomats invariably have expensive German cars.

Next door to my friend lives a tiny old woman whose pride and joy is an overgrown Great Dane. Every afternoon at precisely 1:00 pm, this woman emerges from her dark apartment, led by her giant companion. They cross the street and start down the sidewalk lined with German cars, all equipped with the latest antitheft devices. As the dog comes to the first car, he raises a large leg to mark his territory, and simultaneously activates a raucous alarm. Appearing oblivious to the screaming siren, the woman and her canine accomplice proceed to the next example of German engineering with identical results. They thus proceed down the line of automotive finery, leaving a cacophony of security in their wake.

On the bus home to the Hobbit today, there is a man seated, while a man and woman stand beside him. The man who is standing is having a heated discussion with the man who is seated. Still knowing only a few words of Slovak, it appears obvious to me that the man who is standing is berating the seated man for failing to offer his seat to the woman, who just as obviously is the wife of the man who is standing. While we rattle along, bus stop after bus stop, this argument continues, with the woman occasionally touching the face of the standing man, apparently trying to thank him or console him. Finally, the seated man rises, and heads for the exit. As the bus lumbers to a stop, he gets off, followed closely by the woman, leaving the angry man behind. I have ignorantly given the wife to the wrong husband. Don't ask, I don't know.

THE PEN IS MIGHTIER

After I made some acquaintances here, I asked them how they had persevered during the communist years. No one really wanted to complain about life in his or her own country, however one person finally relented to tell me a couple of stories.

It seems that during the "Prague Spring" (1968), Moscow sent in tanks to stop any sort of progress. After that, the people of Czechoslovakia realized that they couldn't fight the Soviets with force. They turned to the only weapons available: humor and sarcasm. A plaintive plea printed artistically on posters in 1989 was:

> *If Not Now, When? If Not Us, Who?*

The most comprehensive commentary came when people started calling their country:

> *Absurdistan*
>
> *the 16ᵀᴴ province of the USSR*

This is really living by your wits. Ever since, Eastern Europeans have specialized in avoiding confrontation with the authorities through word play, not unlike the master, Shakespeare.

Beaten Off The Path

The next morning it is time for a bus ride with the other professors. This is a tour arranged, presumably, to start our education in European history and culture. We head about one hundred kilometers east of Bratislava to a quaint little village and the Castle on the Hill overlooking the quaint little village.

At least at first glance, it looks like the average quaint little village. Actually, someone has invented a better tourist trap and we are beating a path to her door. I wonder if there is any of Eastern Europe that has so far escaped the fate of "Disneyfication." To twist the imaginative phrase of Lord Acton, "tourists corrupt, and absolutely too many tourists corrupt absolutely."

The castle, however, is magnificent, and the souvenir stands are left behind at the castle gate like so many

Time for a pop quiz, class.
Is this castle in Slovakia?
Or Disneyland?

defeated infidels unable to scale the castle walls. The tour guide speaks only Slovak so I am forced to make up my own narration as I go along. This is great! The planning, architecture and engineering that went into this is truly impressive.

Someone who understands Slovak explains one nice touch to me. There is a large hall where the King had a throne and received his subjects to hear their requests, or not likely, complaints. His throne sat between the only two windows in the room, so that his subjects could not see his face clearly as they spoke to him. They could only see shadows and hear his voice. This is pretty slick politics, even if done by a 20th century spin-doctor.

The more I thought about it, the more it seemed like the way things work today, what with the advisors, experts, commentators, pop psychologists, and anchorpersons (is an anchorperson a real drag?) all telling us what the President REALLY meant, and how we are supposed to FEEL about it all.

About halfway through the castle, our group catches up with the group that started in front of us, and we realize that this tour guide is speaking English. Pretending that we are lost, a few of us jump ship, so to speak, and join the English speaking tour.

This isn't as much fun, as our imaginations are now in neutral, but I do learn why the steps in the castle were built so inordinately high. The designers deliberately made the steps extra tall so that by the time the invading knights had climbed from the gate down below, to the chapel on the top floor, wearing all that heavy armor, they would be too tired to fight. I try, but fail, to imagine how we can apply this lesson to modern warfare.

After the castle tour, we have dinner at a hotel and restaurant down by the river below. This is a beautiful site, but a little overgrown, and little used. Puzzled, I am trying to figure out why they built the hotel on the wrong side of the river (the road is on the other side). A professor, whose native language is not English, mentions that "it is obvious this hotel and restaurant have been beaten off the path." I am about to correct him, when I realize that this is a more accurate statement of what we do to countless small villages and towns in America than the cliché I usually recite thoughtlessly in those situations. This is what happens when you confuse historic conservation with tourist conservation.

Up in Prague, it is so bad that Stare Mesto looks like Fantasyland on steroids. Almost everyone is a German tourist; usually in a group large enough to field two American football teams, with a couple of soccer style kickers left over. They walk down the center of the streets, followed by their bus, which make them look as if a giant mechanical dog is trailing them.

BUREAUCRACY BY ANY OTHER NAME

The next morning, I do the two-bus shuffle over to U Brat to see if there is any progress on my attempts to get the necessities. Almost everyday at U Brat someone comes to me and says, "We have a beeg problem." Today the beeg problem is the telephone I requested for my office.

It seems that there is a phone jack in my office but it is set up for building use only. There are apparently four levels of phone service in Eastern Europe. The first level is like a building intercom, the second level can make calls around town, and the third level can make calls in Slovakia, while the fourth level can make calls outside the country. I request to be upgraded from level 1 to level 2, so that I can at least call Slovak U, but the response convinces me not to hold my breath.

Next I request my extension number, so that people can ask for the number instead of me, which will make it much easier for people who aren't conversant in Slovakian to call me. Not only does no one know the extension for my office, but no one can tell me which telephone number someone should dial to get to my floor, so the extension is a moot (can I say academic?) point.

Another beeg problem is housing. I have been living in the one room dorm/hotel that I call the Hobbit, and I would like to move into town. The Hobbit has a huge, maybe thirty meters in diameter, circular sign on the roof, advertising the VW factory next door. This ten-story building and gigantic lighted sign serve as a navigational aid for commercial airliners flying from Prague to Budapest. Just kidding, but it is so bright that it makes it difficult to sleep.

Since this is the least desirable place to live in the region, the rent is only 2500 Slovak Crowns (about $85.00) per month (for Americans). This isn't quite the cheapest place in Eastern Europe, but I don't want to see the winner of that contest. The Hobbit is the place in Bratislava that is where, to butcher an elegant Robert Frost phrase, "when you have to go there, they have to take you in."

Someone at Slovak U tells me about an efficiency apartment for rent, but there is a beeg problem. The controller of the place doesn't have the legal right to rent it out, and since Slovak U requires a legal receipt, no one knows what to do. I suggest that I pay the rent and then give the bill to Slovak U, providing the receipt.

This suggestion will apparently work, but the guy who "controls" the apartment is not willing to let me see the place until a financial arrangement is reached, and I won't agree to a financial arrangement until I see it.

I call this situation a Mexican Standoff, but I wonder what they call this kind of predicament in Slovakia. Maybe an American Standoff? Possibly a Russian standoff? Don't ask, I don't know.

3

Tennis Maniac

"Man invented language in order to satisfy his deep need to complain."
Lily Tomlin

Svetlana interrupts my daydreaming. "You are playing big tennis," she said, "yes?" Svetlana is the department secretary at U Brat and we are standing in the lobby waiting for the acting director to show up. Whenever the opportunity presents itself, I continue my efforts on the office, phone, and class hours. And teaching assistant, of course!

"You mean tennis like lawn tennis." I said.

"But of course," she said, "Wimbledon, England, the Queen."

"Oh, I play tennis, and I brought my tennis racquet," I said, "but we just call it tennis. What is big tennis?"

"Here we say big tennis for Wimbledon tennis, and small tennis only when playing on the green table" she said.

"Uh," I said, "we call small tennis "ping pong" or sometimes table tennis."

Having no golf courses, the Slovaks have adopted tennis as the national sport (if you don't count soccer, of course). There are several good tennis clubs in Bratislava, along with some excellent young players.

Svetlana wants to arrange a big tennis game for me with her father. She makes a rare phone call, and schedules me to play Freddy at his club. Freddy is what we call a teaching pro, in America. This doesn't worry me too much since he is fifty something, and I have a few years on him. He will be using an old-fashioned communist tennis racquet (whatever that is). He doesn't speak any English, but we both speak a little German, and you don't really need to talk to play tennis. Except for talking to yourself.

After a three-bus shuffle (the tennis club is all the way across town), I find the surprisingly attractive club. It has a circular drive, green grass, a parking attendant, and a car park with the occasional jet black Mercedes and deep-ocean blue BMW. I can even see real clay tennis courts peeking from beyond the ivy-covered fence. Real clay courts are quickly disappearing in the USA, but labor is cheap here.

I tense at the onset of the flight or fright syndrome, as there is a whiff of mafia money in the air. I decide to trust Svetlana when I recognize Freddy from her description of him. "He is," she said, "one hundred eighty centimeters, eighty kilos, and eighty years old" (just kidding Freddy, you don't look a day over 79).

May We Serve You?

Freddy easily recognized me first, as I am probably the first American to show up at this private club since the fall of the wall. Freddy knows I speak a few words of

German so he said "guten tag," and then introduces me to his wife, Olga.

Olga speaks no English, but we exchange pleasantries in our own language, then Freddy and I begin hitting the ball back and forth across the net to warm up. Olga takes up a position at one end of the net, starts picking up the errant balls, and throwing them back to us. *This is great,* I think, *we have a ball girl just like real tennis players.*

It's a little disconcerting, however, as Olga is also fifty something and dressed in a long black coat and black scarf. She looks exactly like one of those East German ice skating coaches we used to see during the communist era, out to obtain perfection from her star pupil, for the glory of the fatherland.

Indeed, as soon as we begin to play a real game, she starts yelling at Freddy, saying something like "do this" or "do that." I can't tell exactly what she is saying; my Slovak is still not that good. During a point, if I hit a drop shot, she exhorts Freddy to run to the net, with much waving of arms and quick little steps. When I lob the ball, she excitedly scampers back, urging him back with her. When he makes an error and hits the ball out of the court or into the net, she sighs loudly and shakes her head, at least disappointed if not totally disgusted.

An observer might get the idea Olga has never actually played tennis herself, but she seems to know exactly how Freddy should be playing. Since Freddy is a teaching pro, and has some idea about how to play, it doesn't surprise me when he starts playing worse and worse and soon loses the first set, 6-1. This bitter setback is too much for Olga, who retires to the bar in the clubhouse.

Also not surprisingly, Freddy plays much better without his coach and wins several games, finally forcing a tiebreaker. After he wins the tiebreaker, we are all set to play a third set, to decide the match.

Here comes Olga, with a big smile, back out on the court, having watched the whole thing from the bar. Olga is still in her East German ice skating coach outfit, and Freddy quite suddenly realizes he has a cramp in his leg, and cannot continue. We play many times after that, but Olga never makes another appearance. Don't ask, I think I know.

GAME, SET AND MATCH

Having found that many of the best students are not going to attend Slovak U this term, we all agree that I will offer classes at the new institution, U Brat, this term, and Slovak U next term. This will give me a great opportunity to compare a new institution with an old, established, not to say fossilized, one. In the afternoon I head over to U Brat, where I have a meeting with the Head of Curriculum (and former Minister of Education for Slovakia) as well as the school administrator, Stasci.

On the agenda is the schedule of the fall semester as well as the teaching methods I intend to use. We first make small talk, as you always do in Slovakia, about what I think of Bratislava and what kinds of things I have been doing so far. I tell them that I had the chance to play big tennis, and I feel right at home here. Then we get to business. Usually, it takes longer to get down to business at a meeting in Slovakia, but they hurry things along in deference to American ways.

I let them serve first. Stasci begins by hitting a slice serve out wide to my forehand by saying, "we would like to suggest that you teach one class to the second year grad students that will meet for three hours every two weeks, and a similar class for the first year students."

I return this serve with a deep cross-court proposal, "I would like to offer one class that meets every week for one semester and another similar class the second semester, I am afraid that one class every other week may not produce the desired result."

Stasci drives my return down the line with a forehand, "this educational system has been in effect since the year 1650, and has worked exceedingly well for the last three hundred plus years."

Putting excessive topspin on my two-handed backhand reply, I hit a sharp angle, "if what you want is more of the same education style that you have had for three hundred years, maybe you don't want me to teach, you can just do what always has been done."

Stasci understands the effectiveness of topspin, and gently under spins a cross-court drop shot answer, "Maybe one class every week for six weeks, and then another class every week for six weeks, would also meet our needs."

I return their drop shot with a little sidespin deep in the corner, "I think that I would be much more effective as a teacher, using western methods of instruction, if the class met two times per week for one and one half hours each time, instead of one time for three hours."

Almost conceding the point, Stasci lobs, "at least if you begin with soft shots to the students and gradually become more demanding, when you see how well they are doing."

I put the point away with an overhead smash by saying "if, as you have previously indicated, many students plan on going on to graduate programs in America, then the time to begin American style education is NOW." I take the point, set, and match.

Or so I thought. The next time we start the competition over from the beginning, as if we had never played a game. This is the prevailing bureaucratic strategy (B.S. for short) of universities. I recognize it from the USA, where the chairman of my department used to say "academic politics are so vicious, because the stakes are so LOW."

We take it from the top, from the point where they have been doing it this way since at least the middle ages, and it was good enough during the communist years, when they both were in school. I probably should explain that the director of U Brat, Dr. Vodicova, who invited me to come to Slovakia, supports new ideas. It is just that some of the old guard can't resist making a last ditch effort to continue the old ways. This is what happens when you confuse ritual with tradition.

Whenever the subject of communism comes up, one of my old professors back in the USA, who is originally from Lithuania, likes to tell the story of a small, brown bird who lives in northern Russia.

Whenever this bird is threatened, it lies on the ground on its back and uses its wings to cover itself up with leaves, instead of flying away. It lies motionless, no matter how long the danger is present, and only when the enemy gets tired and goes away does the bird get up, shake off the leaves, and resumes life as if nothing had happened. Thus, it has survived for generations, and may live forever. He has less faith than the rest of us that the communists are gone for good.

I am hoping that communism is more like the parrot in Monty Python's flying circus, than the Siberian bird. As Monty explained, his "parrot is no more. It has ceased to be. It's expired and gone to meet its maker. This is a late parrot. It's a stiff. Bereft of life, it rests in peace. If you hadn't nailed it to the perch, it would be pushing up the daisies. It's rung down the curtain and joined the choir invisible. This is an ex-parrot."

A Streetcar Named Desire

While riding buses all day and all night, you learn the pecking order, sort of unwritten rules of the road, like there are for ships at sea. When you climb on a bus, if there are available seats (not likely, since the revolution) you can take your pick with impunity.

As the seats fill up, the process of bumping begins, kind of like the last day of qualifying at the Indy 500, where each successive driver takes a shot at replacing the slowest driver in the field, the driver on the bubble.

If an elderly, handicapped person gets on the bus, they clearly have a right to a seat (being analogous to a vessel in distress on the high seas) and anyone will get up and offer their seat. Usually the first person up will be a woman, but not always.

An elderly, but not handicapped, person (a commercial vessel at sea) will elicit almost the same response. Young teenage boys try everything to avoid eye contact so that someone else, again almost always a woman, will get up first.

Next comes a young mother with a baby or pushing a baby carriage (like a sailing vessel). Yet again, almost anyone will offer a seat, with teenage boys doing so grudgingly, if shamed into it.

Still, you gotta love a country where teenage boys will give up their bus seat under any circumstances, voluntarily. Finally, there are the rest of us (like ordinary power boats), who can sit only if no one higher on the right-of-way register is present.

Later, I would see chain reactions, sometimes involving most of the people on the bus. An elderly, handicapped person gets on the bus, thereby displacing an elderly woman (the first up to offer her seat). Then an elderly man stands, offering his seat to the, suddenly standing, elderly woman. Of course, this prompts a middle-aged woman to get up and allow the elderly man to sit. Next, a young woman will rise in deference to the middle-aged woman. Finally, a young man will, perhaps not so innocently, offer his seat to the young woman.

This whole ballet without music plays out prior to the arrival at the next stop, where it can, and frequently does, start all over again. Sometimes, several riders exchange seats almost simultaneously, as if the moves are a complex dance choreographed by chess champion Bobby Fischer.

There are several entertaining exceptions. Some old guys take it as a personal affront if a girl or young woman offers her seat to them. In a futile attempt to prove their youth, if not their virility, they will refuse the offered seat. There they stand, angrily and proudly, even if they are in obvious pain.

Also, and less amusingly, mothers will stand, holding heavy bags, while their strong, healthy child of ten or so sits serenely, oblivious to the world. Finally, a strapping six-foot soccer star of twenty will sit while his girlfriend, in high heels, stands by his shoulder, hanging on to the overhead strap for dear life. Don't ask. I don't know.

Uptown Saturday Night

There is a reception tonight to introduce the newly arrived American professors to the local academics. The location is a recently reconstructed building owned by the Energy Ministry, in a converted wine cellar complete with a domed brick ceiling, just like old black and white movies.

Arriving, I look around for Bogart or Bacall, but I can only find a Peter Lorre look-alike. The famous local group "My Father Had An Accordion" provides Slovak folk music. Most talk is about education, local universities, and politics. A cocktail party is a cocktail party, even in Central Europe on Central European Time.

While we are standing around drinking a local favorite called Slivovitz (which tastes suspiciously like kerosene to me) Ludmilla asks, "have you heard about drinking in Russia?"

"Tell me," I respond.

"Russians love to drink Vodka,"she said,"but sometimes a Russian cannot afford a shot of Vodka. What do you do? Say a shot of Vodka costs twenty cents, if a Russian has only ten cents he turns his hat around backwards. Then he looks around the room until he sees another Russian with his hat on backwards. They introduce themselves to each other, shake hands, become the best of friends, and pool their money to buy and share a shot of Vodka. If a Russian has only a nickel, he turns his hat sideways, looks for three new friends and they all share a shot of Vodka.

"That's ingenious," I said, "but I have heard that in Moscow, many poor pensioners cannot even afford a hat?"

"No problem," Ludmilla said, "the guy without a hat stands by the door holding one, two, or three fingers across his chest. Russians coming in the door, also without a hat, are scrutinized for a similar salute, until the Russians without a hat have enough new friends for a shot of shared Vodka."

"Now I know how to find a friend fast in Moscow," I said.

This prompts another person to tell another story, this time about life in Czechoslovakia under communism. A Czech goes into a neighborhood store and, not seeing a loaf of bread for sale, says to the drowsy clerk, "where do you keep the bread?"

The clerk slowly yawns and, almost too bored for words, says, "You are in the wrong store. THIS store has no milk; the store with no bread is next door."

Naturally, a third story is inevitable. A Czech citizen is arrested and thrown into a jail cell. As he bounces to a stop up against the cell wall, the men already crowded into the cell slowly open their eyes. They interrogate the newcomer, "why have you been arrested?"

Communist entertainment,
before the collapse of the evil empire.

"I have done nothing," he cries, "I am innocent!" "Sure you are," they respond, "we all are. But how many years did they give you?"

"Six years," the poor newcomer sobs, "they gave me six years!"

"YOU LIAR," the old timers shout in unison, "you committed some crime, for doing nothing you only get four years!" You gotta love a country that can still laugh.

Having had more than enough talk and alcohol, I try to find the water closet (restroom). It turns out that most of the WC's in Slovakia (at least for men, I never checked the other one) have a woman sitting at a table just inside the door, her job being to collect the usage fee. Sometimes that was 1 Slovak Krown (each Krown is worth about 3 cents) to use the urinal, and 2 Slovak Krowns (SK) for the toilet. Usually, I put down 2 SK in either case, figuring that the woman would not watch me quite as closely if I have already paid the maximum. Having a woman watch while you use the facility is a bit disconcerting, but it doesn't seem to bother anyone here. Indeed, you soon get to the point where you feel a bit guilty if there is no woman to pay. You get a free ride, so to speak, but at least one person is not earning a living that day.

KITTY LITTER

Later that night, I am out at the edge of Bratislava beginning yet again the vigil of "waiting for the night bus to the VW factory." While waiting for what seemed like an hour at a chilly, deserted, bus stop in the middle of the night in the middle of nowhere, I am adopted by a small, skinny, weak, orange kitten.

Since we are both strangers in a strange land, I pick it up and put it inside my sweatshirt, where it promptly goes to sleep. It sleeps all the way home on the bus. The next morning, the "kitten with no name" is doing better. Now I need to go to the potraviny and get some kitty stuff. Stuff like kitty food and kitty litter. After asking around in some English, some German, and the rest dictionary Slovak, I set off on the bus to the "beeg" pet store.

The shop turns out to be about 3x3 meters and has a few dog collars and a little dog food. The proprietor speaks no English, and kitty litter is not in my dictionary. I do manage to get directions to yet another beeg pet store, and head over there. Same song, second verse. While the average Slovak loves dogs, these same people have an intense hatred for cats, and most people barely tolerate them. Thus, most pet supply shops have only the bare necessities for cats: i.e. nothing.

Nevertheless, I am determined to find kitty litter, so next I head over to Trznica, the big market full of little stalls. Trznica is sort of like a huge indoor flea market where you can find anything, sometimes more than you bargained for. Seeing two teenage girls carrying (what else?) a huge bag of dog food out the door, I ask, still in pantomime, where they found it. They direct me to a small stand that carries pet supplies, even some kitty stuff!

Putting my bag up on the counter, I begin to try to ask, again mostly in pantomime, if they have any kitty litter. You just haven't lived until you try to mime kitty litter in a foreign language, in a foreign country, to a foreign people who don't like cats in the first place.

Imagine you are demonstrating a fundamental feline behavioral instinct, by scratching at the air with your paw, I mean your hand, as if you are covering up the results of one of nature's imperatives. See, you get the idea.

Soon I have drawn a crowd, two teenage boys in particular have found their days entertainment, and they have front row seats. Getting more and more frustrated, I finally decide to admit defeat. As soon as I stop, the boys decide that they have about had enough fun for the morning, and we all start to leave. As I pick up my shopping bag, right underneath it, in front of me all the time, is a big bag of "HAPPY CAT!" We are all happy at this development, so I pay for it and head home.

When I arrive, I feed the kitten real cat food that she "hoovers," setting a new land speed record. Then it occurs to me, if I can't communicate with actual people here, how am I going to get the idea of kitty litter over to the kitten.

Deciding that maybe cats are smarter than the rest of us, I cut one side off the cardboard box I brought with me, and start to pour in the HAPPY CAT. The kitten is across the room, but upon hearing this sound comes bounding over like a miniature, demented kangaroo. Without bothering to look, she takes the last six feet in one jump, squats down, and lets go. She found the litter box four times in the next two hours. Any fears I have are buried, so to speak.

LANGUAGE THEORY

The inability to ask for kitty litter got me thinking about why it is so difficult to learn a new language. The Slovak language maintains the Slavic contrast between short and long vowels (too many to name), three genders (masculine, feminine, neuter), and six cases (nominative, genitive, dative, accusative, instrumental, vocative).

Verbs have two tenses (past and present), and two aspects (perfective and imperfective). Slovak word order generally places the most informative elements at the end of a sentence, often violating the basic subject-verb-object structure. And you thought English was complicated.

When a toddler is learning the language of their parents, they might say something like "don't giggle me." Even though the syntax is somewhat unusual, a listener can sense the sense of the words. However, even a toddler would never come up with a sentence where syntax and sense are independent, like my fractured Slovak.

That kind of nonsense is the province of adults, who learned the structure of one language effortlessly as a child, and then find that no effort is enough when learning another language. As an adult, we can memorize the words, but the underlying patterns of "nouny" words and "verby" words are beyond most of us.

We won't even talk about idioms. Try explaining the following to a non-English speaker: "kick the bucket," "buy the farm," "spill the beans," "bite the bullet," "screw the pooch," "give up the ghost," or "hit the fan." On second thought, don't even try. You will "go bananas."

My colleagues are invariably too polite to inform me that my efforts to speak Slovak sound something like this:

colorless green ideas sleep furiously

to steal an example from Noam Chomsky.

They either guess my meaning from the context, as they would the average two year old, or rely on my pidgin sign language to decipher the cryptograph. The Navajo codetalkers in WWII had nothing on them.

Forget grammar. Let's just consider the simpler case of punctuation. Pop quiz, people. Please punctuate the following sentence:

Woman without her man is nothing.

If you are a man, you predictably came up with the obvious answer:

Woman, without her man, is nothing.

If you are a woman, you probably came up with the correct answer:

Woman, without her, man is nothing.

Now try it in a foreign language and see if anyone can understand anything you say. Anything at all.

Looking into this mess, I find the roots of English are in northern Germany, inhabited by pagans like the Angles, the Saxons, and the Jutes. After the collapsing Roman Empire left Britain in the 5th century, these tribes invaded England (Angle-land), displacing the Celts already there.

Digging deeper, I find the best scholarly analysis is by Dave Barry's Mr. Language Person: "the English language is a rich verbal tapestry woven together from the tongues of the Greeks, the Latins, the Angles, the Klaxtons, the Celtics, and many more other ancient people, all of whom had severe drinking problems."

4

Analyze This

"Explanations should be as short
as possible, but no shorter."
Albert Einstein

Today is the first day of school for my new students, and me. During my never-ending negotiations with the administration, I understood class was to be for three hours, from 8:30 am until 11:30 am; however, it turns out that one hour of class on the schedule equals fifty minutes in the classroom. With a fifteen-minute break:

3 X 50 equals 150 - 15 minutes equals 135 minutes.

From 8:30 am until 11:00 am with a fifteen minute break precisely at 9:45 am, sharp. The bells were imported from a school for the soon-to-be-deaf. This is what happens when you confuse graduate school with army boot camp.

These students are second year grad students in the School of Public Administration. The class is Public Policy Analysis, which is a particularly loose topic even in graduate schools in the U.S. Here, I anticipate apprehensively, it will be like teaching a foreign language in a foreign country, to foreigners. I trust I will be more successful than I was in miming kitty litter.

As I walk into the classroom, I try to assess twenty students simultaneously: some male, some female; some smiling, some not; some in church clothes, some in jeans; some sitting on the front row, some in the back corner. I am relieved to see a western style podium. That barricade, that rampart, that maginot line of defense professors throw into the breach, to delay a frontal assault by the students on cherished ideas.

I plan to begin class by saying that I will be teaching in more or less the same style that I use in graduate school in America. This will include a seminar style, with more class participation, written papers, and oral presentations than classes to which they are accustomed. More original thinking with less memorization and oral examination.

"Good morning," I begin. Nothing is the response. "My name is Dr. Wright," I try. More nothing. "This is a class in public policy analysis," maybe the third time is a charm. Oops, this is what happens when you confuse strategy with tactics. O.K., I give up. I will ask them to introduce themselves, and we will get to know something about each other.

"First," I ask, "has anybody had a class with a western professor?" A few students sitting in the front row appear to shake their head, almost imperceptibly, like someone at an auction who wants to bid on a Rembrandt, but isn't sure they can come up with the money.

I try to explain what graduate school is like in the States; i.e. no three-hour lectures once every other week with an oral exam at the end of the term being the entire grade. Then we go around the room and each student introduces herself and tells a little about her background, for my benefit. In American universities I begin by asking why they are taking the class and what is their "claim to fame."

I want to start getting to know the students, but also I want to hear how good their English is, and how they think on their feet. These students take all their classes together, so they know each other pretty well, and there is a lot of laughing and kidding going on (in their native language, unfortunately for me).

All these students are from Slovakia, each with a degree from a university here, and they range in age from about twenty-one up to about thirty-nine or so (I didn't have the nerve to ask her!). They have exceptionally varied undergraduate degrees: from agriculture to physical education to zoology. And just as many reasons for being in my class. The only ones who seem one hundred per cent sure that they want to be here are the young men who will have to report to the army if they ever leave school.

The students are a little slow to loosen up, but by the end of the class a couple of students have the nerve to disagree, out loud, with something I said. Since this is the sum total of spoken words by anyone in the class, except for answers to direct questions by me, I consider this to be a moral victory.

Mostly it is impossible to read faces, to tell if there is much comprehension, agreement, or disagreement. I guess Prince Metternich was right; the Far East does begin at Vienna. I think to myself, *the Chinese have a lot to learn about the meaning of the word inscrutable.* Later that day, we newcomers compare stories. After hearing the first day experiences of other western professors, I realize it was not as bad as it could have been.

I finish class with a simple story about policy analysis. Several hundred years ago at a castle in Europe, the story goes, the Duchess of Tyrol and her army were laying siege to a Kingdom and were camped all around the base of the castle. For several months, there was still a standoff, with the attacking army unwilling to storm the walls, and the defenders unable to get out to get more food and water.

Finally, the commander of the castle decided to give up, as they were down to their last ox and bag of barley. He told his subjects that they would have to surrender the next morning. During the night, however, he had a new thought. Since he was unable to get more supplies, what if instead he could convince the army camped below to leave?

The next morning, having no other options, he ordered his people to slaughter the last ox, stuff its belly with the last barley, and throw the carcass over the wall of the castle.

It bounced down the steep hill, coming to a stop in the meadow below at the feet of the Duchess and her army. They too, were short on supplies (and equally short on patience) and they interpreted this sign as a gesture of disgust. They thought that the people in the castle had so much food; they were throwing it down as an insult.

Disheartened, the Duchess and her army decide to leave, and try their luck somewhere else. They packed up their bags and got off the property. The moral of this story is, make sure you are asking the right questions before making a policy decision.

What Goes around, Comes Around

After class, I stop by to see Stasci, the administrator, to see if we are making any progress on my requests for a phone, a desk, an email account, etc. "Oh, I am glad you are here," Stasci announces, "we have a beeg problem."

"Tell me," I said, not wanting to hazard a guess.

"You know you have an office for yourself?" she said.

"Yes...?" I venture in a noncommittal way.

"Well, we have just received a grant from a company in the Netherlands to buy a new computer..." she trailed off.

"And...?" I said. Now I can guess what is coming.

"So," Stasci finishes triumphantly, "you must give your office to the computer, the computer must have its own office."

Somehow, I knew what Stasci was going to say. The first clue was that the office next to mine is empty except for a lone copier. Compared to that, giving a computer its own office makes perfect sense.

Knowing that it is useless, I still have to make a token effort to hold my ground. "Uh, Stasci," I begin, "don't you think that the lonely copier next door would be a lot happier if it had a cute little computer to keep it company? You know, two healthy single machines...a little privacy... a bottle of oil...maybe we could get a baby plain paper fax machine out of the relationship?" I know what you are thinking, it sounded just as stupid to Stasci. That's what happens when you confuse the ridiculous with the sublime.

Stasci said nothing. I didn't have a prayer. "So Stasci," I continue lamely, "what can I use for an office?"

"Oh, not a beeg problem," Stasci responds cheerfully, "I have had an extra desk put in the public administration program office, and you can share it with Mr. Pischut, he only comes in three days a week anyway."

GOOD NEIGHBOR POLICY

I have an appointment tonight at 7:30 p.m. to look at an apartment for rent, and it is 6:30 p.m. Later, I will get stood up, but I don't know that now. What I know is that the bus will take at least thirty to forty minutes, so there is no time for a real dinner. Finding a liter of fresh, sweet, cold, milk (a real treat) at a market, I look for a little freestanding stand to get a "langose," a type of fried bread smothered with some type of garlic butter spread. Langose is cheap and filling, and satisfyingly greasy.

My usual langose stand is too far away today, so I look around for a closer one. One is beckoning me from about half a block away, so I head toward it at a fast walk. While approaching the new stand, I have a little informal race with another guy coming from the other direction.

I win by a nose so the loser stands right beside my elbow, watching and listening as I put the liter of milk on the counter in front of me, and try to order. After telling the girl that I would like "jeden" (one) langose, I realize that I am in trouble. At my usual langose stand, multiple choices are nonexistent.

You can only order one thing, one way, kind of like the original Apple Macintosh computer. Here, I realize too late, there is a menu of toppings and the girl wants me to choose one. I can understand what she wants me to do, but I cannot understand the choices. In exasperation at my stupidity, she points to a list taped to the front window. No help, it being, naturally, entirely in handwritten Slovak.

With the sore loser beside me getting sorer and sorer, I resort to a strategy that has worked in other situations where I am trying to order without knowing the language. I point to the list, and say "dobre?" then point to the girl. I am asking "good?" and trying to get the girl to help me out and make the choice, choosing something "good."

She clearly doesn't want to play this game, unlike some waiters who are delighted or amused to help. Finally, with the guy beside me beside himself, snorting in disgust, she spreads some kind of cream on the fried bread and then sprinkles cheese over the whole thing. Relieved to be

The Darth Vader bridge keeps the panelaks of Petrzalka at bay. May the force be with you.

through this ordeal, I pay the nine krowns (about twenty-eight cents) and repair to the far side of the stand to lick my wounds and eat my langose.

The guy who was a witness to this sorry episode gets his langose with no difficulty, a catsup topping. Later, as I learn more local customs, I discover that locals consider catsup a local delicacy, and the preferred langose topping. He comes around the corner of the stand to eat his prize. Since I am standing in the middle of the only available counter, he points to the counter in front me and silently gestures, asking if I will move over so he can share the space. Hoping that he is not too angry with me for making him wait, I move to the end.

For a while he eats in silence, occasionally glancing at me out of the corner of his eye. Finally he can take it no longer and, waving his arms around like a conductor who has misplaced his orchestra, he starts muttering, "dobre, dobre" (good, good) all the while shaking his head in disgust. I can't figure out if he is angry about the delay I caused, or my lack of language, or my asking for help, or maybe the topping that I finally got on my langose. As he works himself into a frenzy, I am getting a little nervous.

Finally, failing to make me understand the seriousness of my transgression, whatever it was, he puts his half eaten langose down on the counter. Walking quickly down the sidewalk, he is heading back the way he came, still muttering to himself.

Breathing a small sigh of relief, I resume my meal of langose and milk. Reappearing about two minutes later, he is carrying two bottles of "pivo" (beer). Picking up my carton of milk and slamming it as far down the counter as he can, he places the bottle of pivo in front of me, saying as loudly as he can without shouting, "dobre! dobre!" and pointing at the bottle of pivo.

The light finally dawns; you just can't drink milk with langose in Slovakia. We share the rest of our langose, and a beer, like two old friends. You gotta love a country where a Good Samaritan will teach you the finer points of dining out.

FACE THE MUSIC AND DANCE, STRANGER

For two weeks, I have been taking the opportunity to attend concerts during the annual music festival. This is my first opportunity to see the Polish Philharmonic, the Vienna Philharmonic, and the Moscow Philharmonic. Not counting all the other world-class orchestras at which you can shake a baton. Where else can you hear the Moscow Philharmonic for 25 krowns (about eighty cents) sitting on the center aisle, row five?

All of the national orchestras are excellent, but one day I decide to take a break from this highbrow, classical stuff, so I stop by an experimental music session. The experimental music is about what you would expect if you let a million monkeys write music on a million typewriters for a million years. O.K., maybe not that good. My best guess is that it is really bad modern German opera sung by a young, obese woman who is accompanied by a skinny bald guy trying desperately to learn to play the accordion right in front of us.

To begin with, he is violating a law that I have been trying to pass in the USA for years: *play an accordion, go to jail.* It would be like the three-time loser law for violent offenders, except we would skip the last two infractions.

This singer has one of those square jaws that seem hinged like a ventriloquists dummy. Now that I think about it, that accordion player was moving his lips all the time...nah, I guess not.

The lengthy experience was mostly my own fault since I violated my own law and got stuck in the middle of a long aisle, so I couldn't leave until the fat lady... well, you get the idea. Trying to avoid dozing off, I glance around to find some other entertainment. I notice the overhead spotlights focusing directly on the accordion. As he is trying to learn how to play, he is squeezing mightily back and forth. Two reflections of light from the overhead spotlights play photon tag across the ceiling and down the walls to entertain the audience until, well, the fat thing happens. The mystery is how this amateur hour act got on the same program with the Vienna and Moscow Philharmonic orchestras. Don't ask. I don't know.

HOME AGAIN, HOME AGAIN

I actually went to look at an apartment for rent today. Ever since I have been at the Hobbit, I have been looking for a better place to live, but I have been looking for all this time without actually seeing anything for rent.

I have heard rumors, usually someone knows someone who knows someone who has heard of a place that might be for rent, especially for a rich American who will, if greedy and stupid, pay twice the going rate. I am desperate enough, but on my local salary I have no choice.

Anyway, this place sounds too good to be true. It is right in the middle of Old Town, and the price is in my budget. Taking Svetlana with me as an interpreter, we head to the medieval part of town. Buildings here are authentically old. Probably the 14th Century, and impressive. The entrance, as is typical, is through an arched walkway into a courtyard. This building was apparently a trolley barn at one time in its life, as there are abandoned narrow gauge tracks leading from the street through the archway, where they disappear into some kind of boarded up warehouse.

The location is spectacular, the requisite sidewalk café is on the ground floor street side, and the price is right (about 3500 SK, or $120.00 per month). The apartment consists of one moderately large room that functions both as a living/bedroom, and as a tiny eat-in kitchen. There is no balcony, if you don't count the hall outside the front door that overlooks the street. I realize this is my only chance to live in a building older than America.

Trying to suppress my glee, I am just about to say *I will take it, is ten minutes too soon,* when something occurs to me. *Where is the bathroom? No, really. No kidding.* I think maybe I just do not understand the language as we try to discuss this. Quite soon, I am quite sure that the bathroom is conspicuous by its absence.

Hold the press, I was wrong, it turns out that there is a community water closet outside and down the hall. This is just a toilet, not even a sink, much less a shower or tub. Svetlana tells them, "he would take it right now if it just had a shower." They said, "no problem, we will put one in the back of the kitchen immediately after he moves in." There really is room for one there, honest.

I huddle with Svetlana. "What are the chances," I ask, "that I will ever see the shower in my lifetime?"

Hordes of stressed out commuters
fight their way home through
rush hour in Stare Mesto.

"How old," she asks me, "is the building?"

"Maybe four or five hundred years," I said.

"Have they put a shower in," Svetlana asks, "during that time?"

"O.K.," I reply, "I guess maybe you could have a point. Can we trust them just this once?"

"Sure you can," Svetlana said, "just stay downwind from me from now on."

"I give up," I said, "please tell them to call me when the shower is in and working." At this rate, I figure it will be about five hundred more years before they call. *What is the person who rents the place going to do?* I think, *or for that matter, how about the hundreds who have lived here over the centuries?* Don't ask. I don't want to know.

CRIME IS ITS OWN REWARD

Contrary to dire predictions from local friends, I have not experienced any crime on the streets. I know a couple of people who have had close calls, and a couple of bags were stolen that were left unattended, but that is all. Today that almost changed.

I was walking through the main square in Old Town, carrying my omnipresent bag. This is the Swiss army knife of bags: book bag, briefcase, tennis bag: the mother of all bags. You think women's purses in the USA are big, with many pockets and hidden hiding places? They have nothing on my bag. Try an experiment. Leave your house on foot, stay out all day, go into several stores and pretend that you can't find what you need, search vainly for a water fountain or a public restroom. Find a park or a tennis court. See how big a bag YOU carry the next time.

While I was wandering around like a tourist, a big young man bumped into me. A shorter, older man accompanied him. The bump was accidental, I think. After glancing at me and my bag, with two expensive American tennis rackets sticking out of it, they apparently decide that they need the bag and the racquets more than I do.

I continue down the street. As is my habit after getting bumped on a busy street in Eastern Europe, I glance back just to make sure that no one is following me. This time they are. I make a quick right turn around the next corner, stop at the first shop window I come to, and wait. There they are, coming around the corner behind me. I go across the street and duck into an open shop door, step to one side and wait. I watch as they come in, again right behind me. As they step into the shop out of the sunlight, they can't see momentarily.

I cut behind them back out into the street, go to the middle of the cobblestone street, and stop, turning around to face the shop door. Out they come, moving quicker this time. Holding my ground, I stare directly at them. Having no choice, they have to walk past me down the street, clearly not what they want to do.

As they go past, I notice that the shopkeeper has followed them to the door and is monitoring their progress, so it is not just paranoia on my part. Talking to each other all the time, they get about thirty feet past me and suddenly stop. Then they turn quickly, and head back toward me.

Running out of open doors, I look for more options. They almost reach me, but using a big man and his wife as a moving screen (illegal in the National Basketball Association) I again get past them. The big one tries to cut me off, but he is too late. I keep walking, keeping the screen between us. Finally, they give up, presumably to find another target. Don't ask. I don't know.

COLLECTING STAMPS

Meanwhile, later that same day in another part of town (I always liked that segue in the Superman comic books),

I am standing in the customs office at the airport. I am trying to retrieve a couple of boxes of textbooks that have been shipped over for my class. It turns out that customs won't release the books without the official stamp from the Foreign Ministry. This is the stamp signifying that the books are verifiably nonprofit humanitarian material. Like there is a big black market in the "used policy analysis textbooks" business.

I can see it all now, a slick, greasy guy in a leather jacket sidles up to a young boy in a schoolyard and says, "hey, kid, wanna score some dope, some vodka, or how about these hot used policy analysis textbooks?"

After trying several different tactics, I finally admit defeat and do the two-bus shuffle back into town to the Foreign Ministry to get the requisite official stamp. This strategy, I'm sure, can't fail.

At the Foreign Ministry, I find that they won't stamp this customs document, they will only stamp an official form from the Education Ministry. With less enthusiasm, I try various tactics here, too. After admitting defeat once again, and heading back across town to the Education Ministry, I am finally in position for another go.

All I need from the Education Ministry is a blank form, take it to the Foreign Ministry, get it stamped, and then take the stamped form to the Customs Ministry to get the "humanitarian aid not to be resold just to use in my class sign over your firstborn" textbooks. Wrong again. The Education Ministry refuses to provide the form. "It is not necessary in this case," the young woman repeats firmly, redundantly, "that law has been changed... that requirement is no longer required." Usually, I am all for requirements that are no longer required.

Apparently the Customs Ministry does not really need this form, they just think that they do. This is a novel twist on the classic catch 22, which involves three players. With no point of entry into the system, I am effectively stymied. Svetlana informs me that this is just another aspect of the meaning of Central European Time. You gotta love a country that goes by the book, so to speak.

In this case, I had a Slovak interpreter, and she had high-level contacts at both the Foreign Ministry and the Customs Ministry. Our fatal mistake was not having a contact at the Education Ministry. Spending the day in a fruitless loop, we head back to the office to plot a new assault on the bureaucracy.

The next morning, I can't come up with a fresh approach that I think has a better chance of working than, say, the chance that rock stars will voluntarily give up drugs and underage girls. So I call old Sigmund Freud up on his cell phone and say "hey Doc, how can I get my textbooks out of customs? These 'by-the-book' mindless bureaucrats are driving me crazy."

Sigmund is in a rare good mood, because he has just invented the fifty-minute hour, and he has an extra ten minutes to snooze before his next patient.

"Vell, let us see," Sigmund declares. "Do you hate your father and love your mother?"

"No, Doc," I sigh in exasperation, "I'm not the problem, THEY are the problem."

"Oh yes," Sigmund agrees. "Vell, I usually only work with wealthy, middle-aged women who hang out in Viennese coffee houses and are sexually repressed, but I vill make exception in your case."

"Thanks Doc," I declare irreverently. Then I mutter beneath my breath, "And your check is in the mail. So," I continue brightly, "What should I do?"

"DO?" Sigmund nearly screams, "DO? You can't do anything for years, we must have deep analysis and discover what happened in your childhood with you and these burrow cats. We must unearth the dark sexual secret that is driving you crazy. Did a wild animal scare your mother before you were born? Have you had many erotic dreams after seeing *The Lion King?*"

"Uh, never mind, Doc," I said quickly, "I didn't mean to say that they were driving me crazy, I meant to say that they were driving Miss Daisy. It was just a slip, Freud."

"What did you say?" muses Freud, "it was just a slip? Hey, call me nuts, but I think we got something here."

CENTRAL EUROPEAN TIME

I have been trying to tell a visitor from the USA about some aspects of what we call Central European Time. This is a multi-faceted concept involving appointments, bus schedules, attitudes, and much more. I will try to illustrate just one aspect of the concept of Central European Time by describing my trip home tonight.

Freddy and I have an appointment to play tennis at 5 p.m. this evening. Between making the date and today, daylight savings time has disappeared, so that it is getting dark at around 6 p.m. instead of 7 p.m. We couldn't call each other (his phone doesn't work), so we wound up with only about one hour to play instead of the two hours that we planned. Using mostly hand signals to agree that the next time we would meet at 4 p.m., I head home just about 6:30 p.m. I live across town, out in the cornfield, about a fifteen-minute car ride, if I had a car.

First, I walk about one hundred and fifty meters to the bus stop. Luckily, a bus is pulling in just as I arrive and I make the connection with a minimum of running. Needing some milk for the kitten, and some stuff for me, I want to stop at a potraviny on the way home, and this bus will take me about 90% of the way to the store (about two or three kilometers).

Since getting a ride 100% of the way would have entailed two buses and yet more time waiting, it was faster to go 90% of the way on one bus and walk the other 10%. This way I get to the store just before it closes at 7 p.m. Most stores, including grocery stores, close at 6 p.m. There are only two stores in all of Bratislava that stay open past 6 p.m., and I was lucky that one of them was on my way home.

Arriving, I have another break. In Eastern Europe, it is customary, even required, for a customer not to enter the store until a small shopping basket (the kind you carry) is available. If all the baskets are in use, the store is technically full, and it is necessary to wait until a customer leaves the store and returns the basket prior to entering. This is no fun at all in the middle of winter. In this instance, there is a basket available when I arrive so that I don't have to wait to get in. Quickly picking up a few items, I get in line. More luck, there are only five people in line ahead of me instead of the usual ten or more.

Moving slowly, I advance relentlessly until I reach the checkout stand. Just as I am about to put my items on the counter, the cashier leans over, points to the floor in front of me, and says "POZOR, POZOR" (danger, danger). She points out that someone in front of me has dropped about a quart of something that resembles ice cream on the floor in the middle of the exit lane, directly between the check out stands. Since no one is making any effort to clean it up, and it is directly between those of us in line and the door, we all troop cheerfully right through it and out into the street.

Now comes a major decision. The trip home from the store requires at least two buses no matter which way I go. Should I take a short, slow, local tram to the beginning of the express bus route, and then maybe have to wait quite a while for the express bus, which does not run as often as the local buses but makes fewer stops? Or, should I take a chance on two slower buses on medium routes, which run more often but make quite a few more stops? Decisions, decisions.

Since I am carrying my bag of groceries as well as my bag of tennis stuff, I opt for the express. This involves fewer stops and thus fewer opportunities for new passengers to require me to shift position. Waiting only 26 minutes for the first tram, I arrive quickly at the beginning of the express route and find that it is not too bad, I will only have to wait about 20 minutes for the bus that will take me most of the way home.

The bad news is that once on the bus, I am unable to find a seat and must stand holding a heavy bag of groceries in one hand, a heavy bag of tennis stuff in the other hand, and the overhead strap with the other hand.

The trip is only about nine or ten kilometers but requires frequent movement to allow passengers to get on and off. The good news is that the express bus only makes about ten stops before getting to the Hobbit, unlike the twenty or thirty stops that the local buses make.

Arriving at the end of the line (literally), I walk another one-half kilometer carrying my two bags. Here I am at the Hobbit, needing only to climb three flights of stairs and I will be home.

Looking at my watch as I go through the door (using my other hand), I see that it has taken me just less than two hours to make the twelve kilometer trip home (about eight miles), including stopping for a small bag of groceries. I am beginning to understand why almost everyone walks almost everywhere.

Not bad for Central European Time; this trip I had good luck all the way. There will be times when the luck is not so good.

5

Buses Are Our Friends

"The only reason for time is so that everything doesn't happen at once."
Albert Einstein

Last night, while having dinner with American colleagues, I told them the story of the kitten with no name and my adventure finding kitty litter. During a pause in the serious laughter at my expense, we got down to the serious business of naming the cat. We went through all the usual suspects for cat names, like Rover and Spot. O.K., so these are not your usual cat names.

We finally decide that there are no standard cat names in America, like Fido or Killer for dogs (fluffy doesn't count). Here in Slovakia, although we have met numerous people with numerous dogs, no one knows anyone with a cat, so we don't have precedents. We couldn't come up with anything except "macka" (pronounced like machka), the Slovak word for cat.

With dinner, we drink "Burciak" (pronounced something like burrrchack and you try to roll the r), which is not real wine, being the first pressing of the local grapes. Burciak is a young, slightly wild, not-yet-wine, mainly orange in color liquid that feels smooth but has a substantial kick. While drinking this potent concoction, we are still trying to come up with a name for the kitten, which is a young, slightly wild, not-yet-cat, mainly orange in color that feels smooth but has a substantial kick. Burciak it is!

Feeling much better now that the kitten, I mean Burciak, has a name I head back to the Hobbit via the obligatory two-bus shuffle. After I get home, and play with the kitten for a while, I feel a little groggy and decide that I have had too much Burciak. This is what happens when you confuse wine with a cat.

Dom Kultury (House of Culture)

Today is Slovak Official Culture Day. I spend it perusing, what else, culture. I begin at the City Art Museum, with obligatory piquant Slovak art. Passing abundant religious artifacts, I find spectacular ancient woodcarvings. Climbing a magnificently wide, magnificently white, curving marble staircase, I come to more recent works.

Art summoned from Hell, commissioned by the Gods of War. Significantly ugly, disturbing images. Gaunt faces with emaciated eyes obliquely searing your soul. Burning black outlines, mercifully missing detail. Unforgettable, formidable features. Depictions darkly depressing, deeply disturbing: dredging deaths depths.

After lingering too long, I attempt to appease the gods of art by immersing myself in the Cappella Istropolitana, a local chamber music group. Using violins, a harpsichord, and flutes the enchanting music of the spheres washes lightly over me. Like the morning sun: brushing, teasing, caressing, kissing, cleansing. You gotta love a city that has the perfect antidote to modern art: Mozart and Liszt in the park.

Awakening from my reverie, I decide to call a couple of new friends to see if they want to go out for pizza. I initiate the search for a public telephone.

E. T. Phone Home

Phones are a beeg problem here. Pay attention class, we are going to have a short course on public policy, with a quiz at the end. First, just finding a phone can sometimes present a major challenge. They are not on every corner as in the USA, and they are never in a building. Instead, they are usually out on the coldest and windiest corner. Indeed, that is the first place to look.

When you do find one, someone is using it. If nobody is using the phone, then comes the third problem. There are two kinds of public phones here; pay phones that take coins, and pay phones that take a prepaid card that is debited as you speak. It is always one or the other, as no phone accepts both. When you find a phone that accepts coins, all you have is a card. When you find a phone that accepts cards, you don't have yours with you.

O.K. class, let's pretend that you find a phone, that the phone is not in use, and that the phone takes whatever form of payment you happen to have on you at that time. Now class, can you make a phone call?

"No," the class answers in unison.

"No? Why not?" I said.

"Ha, ha, ha, the phone is out of order," the class sings in three-part harmony.

"Do not pass GO, do not collect $200, go directly to another corner and start over," I finish.

My personal least favorite situation, in addition to all of the above, is to find a phone that meets all of my criteria but the glass has been shattered all around the booth. When you step in and close the doorframe, the cold wind whistles around you so loudly that you cannot hear. There have been occasions when I have played the entire game, waited in line watching others make calls, only to have the phone not work when my turn comes. Don't ask. I just don't know.

Years ago, I was living just south of Miami in Florida, when Hurricane Andrew paid a visit. After we dug our way out of the rubble, the first thing we looked for was a phone that worked. Just after the worst natural disaster in U.S. history, we had almost the same experience with phones that I have every day in Slovakia.

There was a simple solution in Miami. Like almost everyone else, I drove up to Ft. Lauderdale and bought a cell phone. The solution here in Eastern Europe is even simpler. Since I don't have a car, and there is no Ft. Lauderdale to drive to, I don't make calls. If I want to speak with a friend, it is easier, faster, and less frustrating just to take the two-bus shuffle to see them.

QUEUING THEORY

Speaking of someone cutting in line in front of you, in the USA we call this rude and obnoxious. In Eastern Europe, we call it a philosophy of life. If you must wait in line, you try not to leave the kind of space between you and the person in front of you that is typical for an American line

This would be just enough space to insert your American Express card between you and the next person. If you leave that space here, someone will magically appear in front of you, thus moving you backwards without your doing anything, or even noticing. They never shove you or even touch you, they just somehow teleport themselves through you. Beam me to the head of the line, Scotty.

Watched from the side, a Westerner standing in line who is not adept at queuing in Eastern Europe will appear to move backwards. I have christened this "unintentional moon-walking." Instead of staying in one place, you really do slide in reverse. I call Einstein back to see if this is some kind of weird quantum mechanics at work, but his phone is out of order.

This accidental moon-walking phenomenon happens when you are trying to read a bus schedule, get on a bus, buy a movie ticket, or buy some bananas: everywhere. Imagine you are standing at the counter in a shop paying for your purchase. Someone will come up behind you, insinuate themselves transcendentally in front of you, and try to buy something while you are waiting for your change.

This is not aberrant behavior, don't call Miss Manners or your psychiatrist, this is life. There is no line rage, no one even takes offense. If they do, you can bet they are from the USA.

Bus Stop, The Movie

There is a related phenomenon on the bus. Imagine again that the bus you are on is standing room only, in other words, most of the time. Imagine further that the bus is arriving at your stop. How do you get off the bus? Here, the accepted technique is to moon-walk through the mass of humanity between you and the door before the stop. If you wait until the bus actually stops at the stop to make your move, there is no way you will get off the bus before it takes off, no matter how many people get off and on.

"So, class, having positioned yourself in front of the door before it stops, can you actually get off the bus here in Eastern Europe?" I inquire, "class?"

"No," the class answers in unison.

"No?" I repeat redundantly, "why not?"

"Ha, Ha, ha, people getting on the bus push you back on," sings the class still in three part harmony.

"Just leap into the crowd, and take your chances that you won't get moon-walked back onto the bus in the confusion," I finish.

A relative to this phenomenon is that of "accidentally" getting off the bus. When people pack the bus wall-to-wall, like stoned fans at a Stones concert, the last people trying to get on must stand jammed against the door. Then when the bus arrives at a stop, there is no way for the people who want to exit at this stop to actually get off without someone getting off first, clearing a path.

So, the last people on will have to get off, and if not quick and resourceful, will get moon-walked to the back of the pack waiting to get on. Sometimes it happens that these hapless victims fail to make it back on the bus. We chickens, who stayed safely behind, wave goodbye as the bus pulls away without the unfortunate volunteers. This makes getting on and off the bus at the desired stop a real sport. I expect to see it in the next Olympic games. I don't expect medals for the USA.

INTERNATIONAL SIGN LANGUAGE

One day I ask Ludmilla to write out a few necessary phrases in the Slovak language that I want to learn such as:

"I'm sorry I ran over you with my grocery cart."

"How do I get to the Ben and Jerry's in Brno?"

"Yes, Castle Devin is my castle."

"You are so beautiful, let's get married."

"You stupid idiot, get out of my way, I will get off the bus, and then you can get on."

"Translation for that last phrase is unnecessary," she said.

"Why is that?" I said, confessing my confusion.

At a bus stop, as mass approaches infinity, the space-time continuum is distorted, and time slows. An oblivious girl gets moon-walked.

"Just say it in English," she answers, "because any phrase that begins 'you stupid idiot' is universally understood, a special version of Esperanto for insensitive Americans."

Having given up on the phone idea, I get a mini-pizza and eat it while on the two-bus shuffle over to a meeting of "The Society for the Preservation of Cultural Music and Dance." That, I'm confident, is not the real name, but I can't translate the real name. I like going to these events, partly to support what they are trying to accomplish, but mainly because it gives me a chance to hear something other than incredibly bad American music.

The amazing aspect of bad American music in Eastern Europe is that it is everywhere. Bus drivers are playing radio stations with bad American music, taxi drivers sitting by the curb waiting for a fare are playing bad American music, even teenagers carrying boom boxes down the street are playing bad American music (go figure). If they were playing it so loud that it could pop blood vessels in your head, you would think you were back in New York. The real mystery is why the Slovaks listen to American music at all. Don't ask. I don't know.

Meanwhile, back at the concert, I am not surprised to see Ludmilla sit down at the next table. I seem to see her almost everywhere. I am beginning to see her even when I don't see her, if you know what I mean. "Ludmilla," I ask, "what are all the songs about?"

"Most are about the same thing, sad girlfriends and missing boyfriends," Ludmilla answers, "the remaining songs are about sad boyfriends and missing girlfriends," You gotta love a country that still cares about family values.

Classless Society

My students are late for class this morning, as usual. The class is scheduled to begin at 8:30 a.m., but usually only four or five of the twenty students are there on time. The rest come straggling in during the next half hour, although rarely all make it by then. They inevitably have excellent excuses; however I can't understand the excuses, much less challenge them. They invariably invoke Eastern European stuff.

One day, when only three students showed up, curiosity got the better of me, and I said "class, why are some students always late?"

"The tram failed to appear," said the first one,

"It was required to visit the foreign police," said the second,

"It is impossible to translate," said the third. Don't ask. I don't want to know.

When they do show up, the class divides itself into about thirds. One third speak good English and actually talks in class if I insist, which I do. Another third will not talk in class unless I make them read from the text or their homework, but their English is also O.K. The remaining third will not speak under any circumstances, so I don't have a clue how much they understand, but their friends assure me they really can speak English.

The assignment for this morning was to conduct an interview with someone in Slovakia who is an expert in the policy field the student is investigating. I think the students are at least starting to get the idea that policy science is mostly policy and not much science. Next week, we are going to tackle cost benefit analysis. I tell them to fasten their seat belts.

I tell the student who chose peace in the Middle East that she was exceptionally clever, since the leaders of the PLO and Israel received the Nobel Prize and a ton of money just for saying they were going to work for peace, not for actually achieving it. This is what happens when you confuse rhetoric with results.

A quaint little village in the Tatras.
Ski all day and disco until dawn.
Church is optional.

DISCO FEVER

A couple of days ago, I traveled to a village in the foothills of the Tatra Mountains for a conference. The hotel where we stayed was one of those small, family run, cozy affairs that are so tranquil. It was quiet until 9:00 p.m. when they open a hidden door to a hidden room.

They crank up a Slovak imitation of an early 70's American disco, complete with spinning strobes, pulsing neon, and rafter rattling Barry White records. Stunning girls, in hot pants and thigh high boots, slink through the usual assortment of John Travolta wannabes.

This went on until 4:10 a.m. I happen to know the exact time, because that was when my bed stopped vibrating from the bass amplification. After hours of sleep eluding me, I closed my eyes in blissful anticipation. The local roosters chose this moment to announce that it was time for this ancient village in the middle of nowhere to wake up. I didn't ask the chickens what they thought about the disco music, but there was an egg shortage at breakfast.

This morning, I am on the bus heading to U Brat when three extra big guys accost me. No need for alarm, these guys are flashing little round badges at me. They are the bus controllers. What I want to say to them, but my Slovak is not good enough, is that infamous line from a Bogart movie, repeated in almost every movie made in the last fifty years: "We don't need no stinkin badges."

The public transportation system here is on the honor system. You have two choices: (1) you either use a ticket every time you get on a bus or tram, sticking it in a little punch at the door that makes a particular set of identifying marks; or (2) you get a pass that is good on any bus or tram for a month. This is by far the best deal as it costs only about $5.00 for the monthly pass.

Usually three controllers work together, one stands at each door to make sure no one sneaks off, while the other one checks each persons ticket for the correct punch marks or pass. They O.K. my valid pass, but the young boys just in front of me are not so lucky. The controllers, finding that they have neither a ticket nor a pass, escort them off the bus. The last I see as the tram pulls away are two small boys surrounded by three big guys. Don't ask. I don't know.

THE UNIVERSAL LANGUAGE

This morning, I get a chance to meet my first real capitalists in Eastern Europe. While in the director's office, speaking with the secretary who speaks almost no English (the other one speaks absolutely no English), a knock on the door interrupts us.

Actually, a knock is not actually what happens when someone wants to come into an office in Eastern Europe. What happens is that the person intent on entering a closed door will tap lightly on the door with one hand, while simultaneously turning the knob and opening the door with the other hand. The entire affair being a seamless chain of events. If done correctly, entry is graceful and effortless. Westerners have a difficult time with this.

The people who enter are door-to-door salesmen. This being my first exposure to Eastern European door-to-door salesmen, I ask the secretary to translate.

"They sell a box of knives to cut meat," she translates, "they have a shop where they sell knives, but have extras. They will sell me the knives for less than one half the usual price." I tell her we get the same offer in the USA.

Politely declining their offer, the secretary opens the door for them to leave. "Please," I said to her, "ask the salesmen where the knives are manufactured."

They don't know, but they are willing to open a box and look for the address of the manufacturer. "Made in the USA," she translates. Don't ask. I don't know.

6

My Kingdom For A Castle

"Education is an admirable thing,
but it is well to remember from
time to time that nothing that is
worth knowing can be taught."
Oscar Wilde

Playing tennis with Freddy today, while he was beating me 6-1, he said in an offhand sort of way, "I found a cottage for you to rent."

"Great," I said, "Where is it and does it have a bathroom?"

"Actually," he continues, "the place is not actually IN Bratislava, it is just a short bus ride up the Danube in the quaint little village of Devin."

O.K., he didn't actually say "quaint little village," I coined that phrase. At long last, I finally found a cottage to investigate.

"That's O.K.," I said, "I haven't found anything around here. Is it right next door to castle Devin?"

"How did you know that?" said Freddy. "However, it is not ready for you to move in; it is being reconstructed."

Does that mean it will be ready in my lifetime, I wonder, or *"real soon now," like the latest update of your favorite computer software in the USA?*

When I first asked Freddy if he knew of an apartment or cottage for rent, he replied, "Ah, apartments are problematical in Bratislava." I try to discourage my students from using words like problematical when they really just mean problem, and utilize when they just mean use. In the USA, people utilize problematical ad nauseam. After coming to Eastern Europe, I have at last discovered what problematical really means. As a colleague informed me, it means "forget it, you don't have a prayer of finding an apartment in Bratislava, especially one you can afford on your pitiful salary."

Nevertheless, Freddy actually comes up with a place for me to look at, even if it is not, really, in Bratislava. Since it is a lot closer to town than the Hobbit where I am now ensconced, off I go. I have an appointment with the owner, a Hungarian named Stefan, and his wife, Romana, who is from Croatia. Naturally.

The only thing you can really see across the Danube River from this cottage is Austria, invitingly close, in every direction. Beckoning, alluring, enticing, tempting. What lawyers in the USA would call an "attractive nuisance" in the class action lawsuit they would immediately file. I guess life under communism had some compensation, no lawyers to file frivolous, or any other kinds of lawsuits.

QUAINT LITTLE VILLAGE

When I arrive, after figuring out a new two-bus shuffle, I find an ancient cottage at the edge of this ancient village of three streets. Spending the last five years rebuilding, the owners have also rebuilt a tinier cottage attached to the side. I am eager to see what a real home looks like, since to date I have only seen panelaks. Before any business is done in Slovakia, even private business like looking at a private apartment, first you must sit, talk, and have a glass of wine. Which we do.

The talk is more difficult than the wine, since Stefan speaks Hungarian, Slovak, and Croatian, as well as some German and some Russian and some Finnish, but no English. Romana, his wife, speaks Croatian, Slovakian, German, and some English, but no Russian. I speak almost no Slovak, some high school German, and just enough English to get by. We usually figure out what the other person is trying to say using only three people and four or five languages for each phrase. This slows down the pace of conversation.

After some small talk, and some big wine, Stefan points to the chessboard on the coffee table between us and inquires, "play?"

"I used to play, about a million years ago," I reply.

"I insist," Stefan said. He won't take incompetence for an answer. After some more wine and a quick game, which takes longer than it should because Stefan takes it easy on me, we finally get around to looking at the apartment. Later, I find that like many people here in Eastern Europe, Stefan is an accomplished chess player.

The cottage to rent is tiny, and charming. It used to be a stable or chicken coop or something, but Stefan and Romana have done some fantastically creative things, doing all the work themselves. It is much different from the Hobbit, where I am now living in one tiny room. Here there is a tiny living room, a tinier bedroom, and a tiniest kitchen, connected by tiny halls. By the time we make it through the kitchen, I have decided to take it, especially when we come to the next stop on the tour, an unusually big bathroom.

Here I change my mind, however, as Stefan gets down on the floor to demonstrate that the drain, in the middle of the floor, is not the lowest spot. Thus the water will not drain properly, leaving a large lake in the middle of the bathroom floor after every shower. There is no separate shower; you take a shower in the middle of the bathroom floor. The entire bathroom is a shower, as in a recreational vehicle in the USA. "This is not Stefan's problem," Romana translates, "since it will be YOUR water."

Visions of a perpetual lake occupying the bathroom floor cloud my thinking. Perhaps I will keep looking for a while, and turn to leave. Stefan (fortunately) calls me back pointing to a secret door in the back wall. Beating out an imaginary drum roll, he opens the secret door to reveal my own private, "ta da," sauna. Turning to Romana, I inquire excitedly "when can I move in? Is ten minutes too soon?"

Shhhh, Library Zone

After I get back to town, having a lease in my pocket in the form of a firm handshake, I stop by the U.S. Embassy library to do a little research on the quaint little village of Devin and Castle Devin.

Having a library of books in English right here in old town Bratislava is wonderful. Later, I will read most, if not all, of the books in this library, and it made a big difference to me during the time I spent in Eastern Europe, since I am a compulsive reader. It did make it a sporting challenge that the U.S. Embassy library prohibits a U.S. citizen from actually checking out a book, however.

The American library, with American books, in the American Embassy, paid for with American money, supported by American taxpayers, is not for Americans. It is for Slovaks, naturally. To be fair, an American can go into the library and read the newspaper, a magazine, or even a real book; it is just that an American can't check out a book. Only Slovaks can check out a book. Pop quiz, class. Why does an American embassy library for Slovakians have a guidebook about Slovakia written for Americans?

It took me less than twenty-four hours to get around this silly regulation. I simply gave each of my students a slip of paper with the name and call number of a book I wanted to read, and they checked them out for me. The fact that Slovaks rarely use this facility, as well as the fact that most of the books I read hadn't been checked out by anyone for at least the last five years, didn't bother me at all, all right? Don't ask. I don't know.

What I learned from the books was that Castle Devin is kind of an owner built castle. What I mean is, I looked for the union label, and it wasn't there. It has a kind of "make do with whatever is lying around," amateur look. Whoever built it didn't have an account at the local Castle Depot store where you can buy all the latest castle building materials. You have to admit you have never seen it featured in the magazine Castle Beautiful. In other words, it is not your basic Cinderella Fairy Tale type spectacular castle you see in the movies. You gotta love a castle that looks like something your kid could build in her spare time. O.K., maybe not my kid, maybe Donald Trump's kid.

It is, nevertheless, my castle. I claim ownership for three reasons. First, I have never lived next door to a castle. Second, it is the only castle up and down the Danube within, oh, a kilometer or two. Third, I can't explain it, but there is a magical aura about the place.

The guidebooks said that the "majestic ruins" of this castle, situated on a "massive rock" above the "confluence of the rivers Danube and Morava," have been here since the dawn of recorded time. This is a "strategic position at the crossroads" of the so-called "Amber and Danube trade

If you pour a cauldron of hot boiling oil
from high atop this turret in Castle Devin, it
will set my cottage at the bottom on fire.

routes." Don't worry about it if you didn't understand all of these big words, this is guidebook talk.

It is also the reason why Devin has been permanently inhabited since the early Stone Age. The Celts left tons of artifacts of their large settlement here. The Romans even integrated the castle into the Danube fortification system known as Limes Romanus. During the time of Greater Moravia in the 9th century, it was called Dowina. Napoleon largely destroyed my castle in 1809.

Destroyed by Napoleon? Wow, I think, this is great! My little cottage, being right outside the gates of what is left of the castle, is where Napoleon probably parked his horse or took a leak. When I first arrived in Eastern Europe, I had a fantasy about living in a place that Napoleon ravaged, and I thought I was just kidding. No kidding, the first thing I did after I moved in was to put up a sign over the door that reads:

> # NAPOLEON SLEPT HERE

I can't prove that he did, but you can't prove that he didn't, either.

There was no way that Napoleon would remember demolishing one little castle during his castle obliterating career, but I called him up on his cell phone because I had a couple of other questions.

"So uh, Mr., Bonaparte, or uh, well, uh Emperor, Sir," I begin, "look, is it O.K. if I just call you Napoleon?"

"Sure, kid," Napoleon replies, "everybody does." It's cute the way he calls me 'kid,' even though I am probably a lot taller than he is.

"Well, uh, Mr. Napoleon, Sir…" I am fumbling around here because I haven't talked with all that many world conquerors. "So, how about those Russian winters, are they brutal or what?" I finally get something out.

"You don't know the half of it, young man, I was having a lot of trouble keeping my tarts from freezing," Napoleon sighed.

"Your tarts?" I rejoin, thinking, *wanton French girls?*

"Oui, my tarts. By the time my baker would ship a cartload of tarts from Paris, most of them would be frozen solid," Napoleon cried. "They were only good for cannon fodder after that. Those frozen tarts really put some holes in the walls of the Kremlin, I'll tell you."

"That's nice, uh, Napoleon, but I wonder if you could tell me why you did it, why you conquered everybody." I continue, "You were everywhere, all over Europe, North Africa, Russia. People even thought you were going to come across the Atlantic and conquer the new world after you finished off the old."

"Why, you ask why?" Napoleon said, "I'll tell you why. That was what the people wanted. I kept getting invitations on my fax: *come and conquer us, we really love the way you ravage a country.* What could I do? They asked for it," he declared.

"I'm not sure that I understand that," I respond weakly.

Napoleon said, "It is simple, you peasant, simple."

"Simple for you maybe," I mutter under my breath, "but for me, Napoleon, complex."

Back At The Farm

The next morning, after arriving to do battle at U Brat, I find that I have a notice from the post office that I have received a package from the USA, but I must go to the Customs office to pick it up.

I inquire of the department secretary, "why must I go to Customs?"

The USA could adopt a few qualities
from Slovakia. For example,
Stare Mesto doesn't need litter laws.

She answers, "if the package has new items in it, you will be required to pay a beeg import tax, since they know you will sell the items." I happen to know that the package contains a bunch of new, made in the USA, tennis balls. I have been unable to acquire good tennis balls here in Eastern Europe, so I figure I am in beeg trouble.

Taking along a Slovak friend for help and protection and translation, we do the two-bus shuffle over to the postal customs office, which is at the main train station, naturally. Upon arrival, we play the universal "fill out this form and go to the next window" game for three rounds. Then, having won all three rounds, we advance into the inner sanctum, where each person has their own official stamp. Upon receiving this stamp, I will avoid the tax.

These stamps are the metal kind with wooden handles, which you use by placing the stamp on the object to receive official sanction, and push smartly down on the handle. This rotates the stamp from the inking pad and whacks it down on the object, imparting a reasonable facsimile of the official seal of Slovakia.

There follows a long conversation in Slovak that I try but fail to follow, about why I could possibly need one dozen cans of new, made in the USA, tennis balls. "It is not possible that you plan to use all these yourself," the officer said in Slovak, "therefore you must be planning to sell them."

"He is a tennis maniac," my translator replies, "and, believe it or not, actually uses NEW tennis balls once in a while."

I do understand the "maniac" part, since maniac means maniac all over the world.

This statement meets with complete disbelief, as everyone in Eastern Europe knows that you never open a new can of tennis balls unless, and until, you manage to lose all the old balls. The concept of tennis balls getting old, losing too much pressure to bounce, wearing out requiring replacement, generates gales of laughter from everyone in the room. I join in. We laugh so hard that one officer loses his grip on his stamping gun and it falls to the floor. Everyone else quiets down and reaches down to touch their stamp gun, just to make sure it is still there. You probably think I am kidding about this.

My friend finally convinces them that there is just no understanding the behavior of crazy Americans. The officer we have been dealing with apparently can believe this, and decides that she will release the package to us, after all. First, however, it requires the obligatory official stamp providing official grace.

Now it becomes obvious our officer is a rank amateur. Looking around for her stamp gun and not seeing it, she reaches across her desk to the desk adjacent for a stamp gun that is just sitting in the middle of the desk. Before her hand closes on the handle, from out of nowhere swoops the owner of this particular stamp, snatching it from the grasp of our officer. The owner twirls it around his finger, like a gunfighter in the Old West and smoothly drops it in the leather stamp holster that I suddenly notice everyone is wearing on her hip. Our officer, clearly embarrassed, vainly tries to explain that she has misplaced her stamp gun and just wants to borrow his for a minute. After all, all the stamps are official and exactly alike.

No. No way. Not in my lifetime. Not over my dead body. It is clearly impossible. I am just about to despair of ever getting my one dozen new, made in the USA, cans of tennis balls, when she changes strategy. Properly chastised, and learning her lesson, our officer sets off on a search to find her own stamp gun. Fortunately, it is located, the package is stamped, and we leave.

Later, I have a long talk with a Hungarian professor of history about the stamp collecting. He explains that the Hapsburgs may not have invented stamping but they surely perfected it. Now it is their primary legacy. After a bottle of Burciak, we mutually conclude that the stamp collecting behavior, especially the territorial aspect of the stamp gun, is a case of "stamp gun envy." Everyday in eastern European officialdom, you see stampers comparing stamp guns to see just who has the biggest one. Don't ask. I'm sure I don't want to know.

Mirror Image

On the way back to the university, we accidentally get on a bus that has empty seats. Enjoying this rare treat, we sit down and, freed from having to hang on, can actually enjoy the scenery and look at the other passengers.

My gaze focuses on two young girls, sitting facing each other on the other side of the bus. They apparently don't know each other as they are not speaking, and are trying to avoid eye contact. This is difficult, since they are facing each other about two feet apart. I keep looking from one to the other. The girl facing forward, on my left, has her left hand bandaged. This would not be remarkable in itself, but the girl facing her, who looks remarkably like her, has her right hand bandaged in exactly the same fashion.

From my perspective, it looks just like a mirror image, I don't know which one is real and which the reflection. Catching one girl's eye, I smile and point from the bandage on her hand to the identical bandage on the other girl's hand. Suddenly they both realize what is entertaining me and simultaneously break into laughter. The girls hold up their hands, and when the other passengers figure out what is going on, soon we have the entire bus shaking from laughter. The poor driver thinks we are all maniacs.

Many organizations over here, including U Brat, have added a technological wrinkle to their operations: email.

Everyone possible has set up an email account, including me. Since the phones are such a beeg problem, this is a welcome and useful development, relatively quick and cheap.

Not only that, we use what is called a "list server." Say you want to send a message to, for example, all the American professors in our organization. You just send it once, to the list server address, and it forwards automatically to everyone on the list. Some people have not quite mastered this technology, and when they try to send a personal message to a friend in the next country, they wind up sending it to all of us on the list server. These personal messages, traveling all over computer networks in Eastern Europe, quickly become a major source of entertainment and amusement to the rest of us, and embarrassment to the sender.

Not everyone, naturally, thinks this technology is wonderful. Yesterday, a fellow professor called me (mirabile dictu) on the phone from Romania and asked me "where is the class material you promised to send me?"

"I sent it to you a couple of weeks ago," I replied, "as an email attachment."

He sighed resignedly and said, "I never seem to get anything on my email. Is it still possible to get it on paper?"

Shopping At Warp Speed

As I am heading to the potraviny this afternoon, a brand new speeding BMW almost runs me over. I can usually jump quickly enough to dodge a Skoda, or amble out of the way of the odd Lada, and anyone can avoid a Trabent. BMWs, though, simply materialize around the corner as if Capt. Kirk has your exact coordinates on board the Starship Enterprise, and when he beams it down, it is already doing warp seven.

Unlike in the USA, where most drivers will usually try to avoid hitting a pedestrian if it is not too much trouble, here we seem to be targets of opportunity. You might even say that Eastern Europe is a target rich environment, from the driver's point of view.

"O.K. class, we are going to have a multiple choice policy quiz. Which of the three answers below is the actual traffic law in Slovakia?

(a) Everyone goes exactly where he or she wants to go, and whoever gets there first has the right of way.

(b) Anything on wheels has the right of way over anything with feet.

(c) Whoever blows their horn first has the legal right of way.

Class? 'c' you say? Actually, unlike some South American countries, the correct answer is 'b'." This seriously reduces your liability insurance bill, and turns the majority of lawyers into advocates for the homeless, because they are one.

You are taking your life in your hands when you enter this demolition derby, and there are wrecks galore. My only theory on the inability of Slovaks to drive either cars or carts in a way that respects the sanctity of human life is that few people here have ever actually driven anything in their life. Walking, buses, trams, and the occasional taxi are the only ways to get around. When they do get a hold of the business end of a car or a cart, the rest of us run for the hills.

"So, class, the only question left on the quiz is, who has the right of way between a shiny new 3,000,000 SK BMW and a rusted out, dented up shopping cart? This is a trick question, because they both have wheels. Don't ask. You already know.

7

Castle Envy

"There are some things so preposterous that only an intellectual could believe them."
George Orwell

Napoleon's ex-cottage, my new home, is wonderful. No stairs to climb, no elevator to avoid, no one room flat buried deep in a panelak, no waking up at 4:30 a.m. to the sounds of the auto factory outside my window.

Now I wake up at 4:00 a.m. to the sounds of guys leaving to go to work at the auto factory. Also, the local roosters and dogs wake up about this time. Of course, I still have to do the two-bus shuffle to get to U Brat or Slovak U. Bus #29 from my house to Old Town is rarely crowded at this time of year, and usually on time, since it begins here and ends here. It seems like I am always living at the end of the bus line.

More good news. Burciak is coming along and is going to be a garden cat. This means that he is not allowed in the house but plays outside all day, and then shows up every night demanding food. We are in heaven. There is a downside, of course. There is a total lack of a public phone in this village, as we apparently live in a phone free zone. There must be some kind of law against having a phone in a designated quaint little village.

The other beeg problem is the frequency of bus #29. During rush hour, when there are more than three of us on the bus simultaneously, bus #29 runs a respectable twenty-five minute schedule. Before or after, this drops to forty to forty-five minutes between buses, when I am usually the only paying rider (we don't count the ever-present girlfriend of the driver.) After 7:00 p.m., the frequency drops again, to one bus every couple of hours. When it shows up.

This makes getting to and from town, as we say in Eastern Europe, problematical. It is not so bad during the warmer months, but later, during the middle of "zima" (winter), I will have many hour long plus waits in the freezing wind to curse the day I moved to Devin. This one horse, I mean one bus, town, is charming and picturesque,

Communist elevator,
before the collapse of the evil empire.

but isolated. This is what happens when you confuse life with a vacation.

Much later, after the spring thaw, I learn that there are hiking trails in the hills above the quaint little village of Devin. Actually, I discover a trail that goes right from my house over the hills to the "Dubravka" area of Bratislava, the home of U Brat.

I hike over in the morning, instead of struggling with the two-bus shuffle. It is a nice stroll through the woods, straight up for about thirty minutes, and then straight down for about an equal amount of time. I figure it is about five kilometers, but if it has rained recently, the ankle deep mud slows me down a smidgen. I wonder if the old Chinese saying is true, that no man can step in the same river twice. I don't know about that, but I do learn that you can step twice in the same muck, yuck.

This morning walk quickly becomes a routine, a chance to avoid the bus, the tram, the smog, and the noise. All I hear are the birds singing, and all I see are deer and rabbits, with an occasional Chinese pheasant. As I walk, I think about what it was like living here along the Danube for the last thousand years.

Try to imagine what this river sees as it falls out of the Alps, near Zurich in Switzerland. First, it heads down through Germany by Munich, speeds through Austria by Vienna, and slows down through Hungary to see the twins of Buda and Pest. Here the Danube turns south through the former Yugoslavia to Belgrade, and curves through Romania around Bucharest. Finally, it meanders through the delta to empty into the Black Sea north of Istanbul, in Turkey.

I can hear the river trying to communicate with me: murmuring, gurgling, mumbling, babbling, chattering, jabbering, and roaring. Being an American, I don't speak the language. Austria is a tantalizing par five across the not-blue-anymore Danube, but only a short par three across the much narrower, but still not blue, Moravia River. Even the pensioners here cannot remember a blue Danube.

Here in Devin, the Moravia River is one border with Austria, but further north, it is part of the border between Slovakia and the Czech Republic.

During the communist years, Devin attracted a certain notoriety as a favorite locale for potential defectors. Oops, I mean of course, criminals who endeavor to leave the glorious homeland of our fathers without bothering to go through the proper procedure of first obtaining an unobtainable visa.

HISTORICAL STUFF

You can skip this part if history puts you to sleep, but I had to learn it so I'm going to inflict it on you, too. In days of yore, there were just two jobs available: hunter-gatherer or castle construction. When you went down to the local employment office, they gave you an aptitude test to see if you were better at killing or building.

Anticipating the need of Napoleon to act out like an average two year old, the local princes offered incentives for their people to work lugging large stones up the hill. It was kind of like a rebate for a new computer. Pay now, mail in the form, and wait the rest of your life for the Czech to show up.

As a matter of fact, lugging big stones was old hat to old Europeans. Predating even the Egyptian pyramids, big stones called megaliths were being carted all over. From the Black Sea, to Malta, to Ireland huge blocks of stone are found in temples and tombs, in rows and circles. Like Stonehenge, for example. They probably had their version of crop circles, too, but supermarket tabloids hadn't been invented yet, so we don't know for sure.

While Paleolithic artifacts have been found dating back thousands of years, the Slavic people only settled in the Danube river basin about 600 B.C., just an eye blink in geologic time. They were getting along fine, acting as a human buffer between the Huns and Western Europe. Attila was steamed, and he beat up on them every chance he got. Since no one seemed to be in charge, the Romans saw an opportunity for more tribute, and set up tollbooths along their side of the Danube.

ROMAN AROUND

Like Napoleon later, the Romans were everywhere earlier. Even along the Danube. Here the Romans finally gave up on conquering everybody everywhere, and drew a line in the sand.

They built a whole series of outposts, designed to protect civilization (i.e. the Roman empire) from the barbarians at the gate (i.e. the rest of us). The Limes Romanus, as the Romans called it, followed the Rhine and the Danube as far as possible. A big river is a cheap fence.

While the Romans didn't last too long in this area (et tu, Brutus?), they did leave some fascinating stuff behind. Fifty kilometers west of Bratislava, underneath Vienna, a substantial Roman legionary camp is preserved. The site is hard to find without a guidebook, as access is through an unmarked door on a side street. I had a tourist map and still walked past it three times before I found it.

Down some steep stairs, under the city, are ruins containing complete systems for delivering water and removing waste from the officers' quarters. Amazing stuff from two thousand years ago. There are cities in the world today that could use that technology. Maybe the Romans really did invent civilization, as they claimed. Nah, they just copied it all from the Greeks.

Historically, there were three distinct areas in this region: Bohemia, Moravia, and Slovakia. Around 800 AD, this entire area was the Great Moravian Empire, formed by an alliance of Moravians and Franks under Charlemagne. This unlikely alliance got together to drive out the original invaders from the East, the Huns and the Avars.

These were the barbarians, who had taken over from the Germanic tribes, who had kicked out the Celts. The revered tradition of evicting former residents with extreme prejudice is a long one. Today we call it ethnic cleansing. This is what happens when you confuse possession with ownership.

This region has always been the crossroads between East and West, both political and religious. Politics and religion being the most famous Siamese twins of history, joined at the hip.

The Pope was intent on spreading the gospel east, while the Patriarch of Byzantium was just as keen on heading west. Here was yet another opportunity for the current king to cash in from both directions. The main guy of the time, Ratislav, had a sweetheart deal going with Byzantium. His nephew, however, made a secret bargain with the Germans, and conspired to capture and blind his uncle.

I guess this kind of history explains why the Eastern Europeans eagerly watch the television soap opera Dallas so much. The popularity of Baywatch remains a mystery, as beaches in Eastern Europe have always been topless.

There is a legend that before Ratislav lost his eyesight, he appealed to the Pope to send a Bishop to convert heathens to Christianity. The Pope, otherwise occupied selling indulgences, ignored the plea. Going to Plan B, Ratislav sent a letter to Emperor Michael III of Byzantine writing, "We, the Slavs, a simple people, have no one to teach us the truth..." etc., etc, etc. The emperor fell for this line, and sent two apostles, actually brothers, who claimed the credit for developing the Slavic alphabet and establishing a university in the area.

The Russians, as ever, have a different version of history. They claim that a Russian prince, the Viking Vladimir, decided to check out various religions and pick one, possibly to use as the opiate of the Russian masses. Ya think?

Legend has it that he sent out survey teams to find the most likely religion, and on their return, let them argue it out in public. Survey Team 1 said, "Bulgarians smell bad." Survey Team 2 said, "Germans have nothing to offer." Survey Team 3 reported, "Muslims are out because they don't allow alcohol. Survey Team 4, sent to Constantinople, was the winner by default. Concerning Constantinople they swooned, "we did not know whether we were in heaven or on earth. For on earth there is no such splendor or such beauty, and we are at a loss to describe it. We know only that God dwells there among men."

God only knows what would have happened if the Muslims had given thumbs up to vodka. Maybe today Russia would be the largest Muslim country in the world. A truly comforting thought.

HISTORY MYSTERY

The Catholics in the region were going great guns for a while, until the next invasion from the east. This one was the particularly successful Magyar (Hungarian) Invasion of 896, which laid the groundwork for many of the current problems. No, really, stay with me on this.

After this conquest, Protestants dominated Slavs to the west, while Slavs to the east found themselves under the thumb of the catholic Magyars. This separation, a primary factor behind the distinct differences between

Czechs and Slovaks, led somewhat circuitously to the breakup of Czechoslovakia in 1989.

The Serbs, the Croats, and the Muslims of the former Yugoslavia are still using approximately the same logic. In school, every schoolboy learns that the assassination of Archduke Ferdinand in Sarajevo started WWI. Actually, no one cared what happened to the hapless Archduke.

What actually happened was that the dual monarchs of the Austro-Hungarian Empire wanted an excuse to demolish the Serbs, who were particularly obnoxious at the time. What Vienna didn't know was that the Germans wanted an excuse to blitzkrieg France, before the French allies, the Russians, could mobilize.

The Germans told the dual monarchy "go ahead, start a war," thinking all the time, *we will finish it.* This was not the first or last time the Germans seriously miscalculated, maybe it's in their pure genes. The European Union is still facing the same problems today: the Germans, the French, and the British all want to be in charge. They each believe that they are the only true natural born leader. Italy would like to think the same, but as Bismarck famously remarked, "she has a big appetite, but poor teeth."

I know what you are thinking; those dull history, geography, and foreign language lessons in high school finally paid off.

HANGING AROUND

Curious about contemporary conditions in this ancient arena, before I left the USA I called a former professor of mine who grew up in what used to be Yugoslavia, to ask what it would be like living in Eastern Europe.

"Zeljka," I said, "what will it be like living in Eastern Europe?"

"The Slovak Republic is the newest American wannabe," Zeljka replied. "It's a former communist country that really doesn't know democracy from a hole in the ozone."

"Do they know anything at all about Americans?" I said.

"They know American movies, and they get Rambo and Bart Simpson on satellite TV," Zeljka said. "Have you ever seen reruns of the old television show Green Acres?"

"Probably," I said, "but not intentionally, why?"

"They watch it every day," Zeljka slam-dunked my apprehension.

Back in the quaint little village of Devin, shortly after the freezing temperatures of the cold war closed the border, the authorities virtually closed the village. Only Devin residents with a special pass could get through the roadblock at the edge of Bratislava. The castle ruins, closed and locked tight, were even more inaccessible than

Man's best friend. This one is unmuzzled,
just in case he wants to bite you.

the village. No one could visit here, much less move here. The quaint little village of Devin would eventually die of old age, if the communist regime lasted long enough.

This state of affairs lasted until 1989. Meanwhile, there were several twenty-foot high barbwire fences along the riverbanks, and guards patrolled the whole area constantly with machine guns. Even worse, they patrolled with real German shepherds. We are not talking Rin Tin Tin here. We are talking the kind of sociopath canine that you see in movies about WWII. The dog about which you have nightmares. The sort of dog that demonstrates how far man can go in un-domesticating man's best friend. My guess is that they had a puppy-from-hell mill somewhere in East Germany that cranked out litter after litter, ready to train as canine Mafioso.

You may well wonder if there were land mines around my cottage, as there was almost everywhere else in Devin. Don't ask. I'm afraid to know.

One day in 1976, the communists were in a good mood, since no one had managed to escape through Devin in a while. They decided to open the castle ruins for a few days. They billed this as a great cultural party brought to you through the magnanimity of the communist party. The first day the castle was open to the public, unfortunately, some ungrateful dissident (maybe the local Wright brother?) took the opportunity to launch himself off the top of the castle wall in a homemade hang glider. He made it across the river to Austria. Devin was locked down again, and sealed tight for the duration.

HOUSING AND URBAN DEVELOPMENT

Many of the cottages in Devin are currently undergoing reconstruction. I guess that during the communist years, you not only couldn't come to the quaint little village of Devin, you couldn't get any building material here, either.

You hear a joke, sometimes, that the brick-laying gene is missing from people east of Vienna. It's true that you never actually see a brick building here in Slovakia, but during reconstruction, you do get to see bricks as they are laid.

Slovaks cover up all bricks with some kind of stucco, and hence see no reason to waste artistic talent during bricklaying. Consequently, they throw the bricks up haphazardly, as if a small child were in charge of construction. Kind of like a brick version of a kid's first tree house, with boards sticking every which way. You might wonder how these walls stand for days, much less years, decades, or even centuries. Then you notice that the typical wall is three or four feet thick. I guess they haven't updated the local building code since the castle building days of the fifteenth century.

Every house stands at the front of the lot, butting up against the road, as close as it can get. If they were any closer, you would have to go through the neighbor's kitchen to get to the bus stop. Even new houses are located so that your shoulder grazes the windows as you walk along the street. I learned this lesson one day when a real German Shepard sitting in an open window tried to bite the top of my head as I walked along the sidewalk. I would have called 911 to get my heart restarted, if my cell phone worked.

Probably the communists didn't have a problem with peeping toms. Frontage not taken up with house is always occupied with an eight-foot metal fence. This collectible of communism has the dual function of keeping everyone out and the guard dogs in. If you wondered what happened to all those real German shepherds guarding the iron curtain, well, now they are guarding every house in Devin.

My theory is that the primary reason for building as close as possible to the road is to save every possible square centimeter of land for the ubiquitous garden and courtyard out back. Every cottage in Devin seems to have a little mini-farm out back. Only when invited through the gate into the inner sanctum, do you appreciate the efficient design that does more with less: a minimalist culture. Who said Karl Marx got everything wrong?

The Village People

Every village in Slovakia has its village characters, just like every small town in America. Here in Devin we seem to have more than our share. We have the flower lady who, like the log lady on Twin Peaks, carries the objects of her predilection with her wherever she goes. They are always fresh, never wilted. How does she do that?

We have the town drunk, the guy who never seems to work, but always seems to have money for booze. At least he has enough money for one more bottle of Slivovitch or Becherovca; or at least a bottle of beer. It is substantially cheaper to be the town drunk here, since a drinkable bottle of beer starts at about 15 cents.

We have the kamikaze kids on bikes. There is an old saying that goes something like if the only tool you have is a hammer, everything looks like a nail. Here the kids with new mountain bikes think every object is a mountain. They like to ride up hills and down stairs. They jump the curb, do wheelies on newly planted lawns, and scream past you so close you can feel them, and not telepathically. You may wonder where they get the money for a new mountain bike for every kid in town. Don't ask. I don't know.

We have the mothers with strollers. If you thought the mountain bikes cost a pretty krown, you should price one of these baby limos. A fleet of these vessels pushed by newly minted moms brings to mind the Spanish Armada. It takes three men and a boy to lift one of these SUVs up on the bus for the daily jaunt into town. These things have an air pillow, ABS brakes, four-wheel independent suspension, rich Corinthian leather upholstery, and a full Bose™ sound system. The only thing missing is the obnoxious burglar alarm. You know the one, when you walk by the stroller a metallic voice threatens you, "stand back from the buggy, you are too close. Stand back from the buggy; an armed kid on roller blades is on the way."

We have the day laborers that come at dawn's early light to work on the reconstruction of Devin cottages. They all have identical overalls and they are at the potraviny at 6:30 a.m. when it opens to buy the first beer of the day. They are at the potraviny at 6:30 p.m. to buy the last beer of the day. I don't know how much beer there is in the middle of the day, let's just say that they put in a ton of hours.

We have the yuppies that live in the quaint little village of Devin but work for a western firm in beautiful downtown Bratislava. These are the suits riding the bus to town; in New York, they would be riding the commuter trains, but you get the idea. There is no Westchester for the yuppies to move to around Bratislava, so they are taking the hard currency they get from western firms and buying out the Devin Village People. Soon the quaint little village of Devin will be awash with IBM salesmen driving their blue BMWs, instead of pensioners riding the bus.

We have the gardeners and the gardener wannabes. These are the people out leaning on a shovel in the middle of their garden about sixteen hours a day. They must do some weeding, digging, and planting because stuff grows in their garden, but you never actually see them doing any actual gardening. They are always available for a long chat about which vegetable they planted when and where, and some local gossip about which villagers couldn't grow a tomato if their salsa depended on it.

We have the retired gossips on pensions. These are the same people who were bona fide gossips their entire lives, but now that they don't have to go to work everyday, can dedicate their entire waking existence to discussing the finer points of neighbors' lives. They particularly love to diss any foreigners (like Americans) who happen by.

We have village dogs everywhere, at least twice as many dogs as people. Every cottage has at least two dogs, and usually three or four. One inside yippy little lap dog; one outside big bruiser guard dog. I happen to love dogs myself, but sometimes there are too many dogs here, even for me, like when they all bark at once.

Most are German dogs like shepherds and wiener dogs, but there are also Russian hounds, French poodles, English spaniels, Chinese pugs, Swiss St. Bernards, Dalmatian Coast Dalmatians, and mutts from the USA. We could field our own canine United Nations. Since every house is surrounded by a tall fence and equally tall gate, you would think that this would be a perfect place to let a dog have the run of the yard, but no. Many dogs are wearing a muzzle, chained up, inside the fenced yard. Don't ask. I don't know.

On weekends, all of Bratislava comes out to drink beer and wine in the shadow of my castle. Literally, dozens of "summer only" beer gardens magically appear on the first day of May. All around the castle, every cottage puts out some sidewalk tables, umbrellas, and a big sign for 'pivo' (beer) and 'vino' (wine).

No problem with all these weekend drinkers, except it makes actually getting on the bus problematical. If you recall, here in Eastern Europe problematical means it can't be done. Many locals (including me) resign themselves to walking the three or four miles back and forth to Bratislava on spring weekends. You probably think I am kidding about this.

8

Exam Time

"Can you do addition?" the White Queen asked,
"What's one and one and one and one and one
and one and one and one and one and one?"
"I don't know," said Alice, "I lost count."
"She can't do addition," said the Red Queen.
Alice in Wonderland

It is exam time at U Brat. I can't believe the term went so fast, but we do operate on three short terms instead of the usual semesters. My students are past ready, as they are used to three days between exams.

Actually, I can't bring myself to give an oral exam, as is the norm here, so I have assigned a short paper. I provided a generic outline so it is kind of like verbal paint by numbers. Going by the kind of questions this assignment generates, these students are getting a Masters degree, and this is the first paper they have written in their academic careers. Well, maybe the first paper in English.

They don't have time to do real policy analysis, so they are going to do a quick policy issue survey, kind of like a position paper for a political candidate. I let them choose the topics, and they range from the privatization of the housing market to drugs and, my favorite, brain drain.

We spend the last few classes working on these papers, and correcting spelling and grammar. They are also learning to think critically, and question authority. This last area is the biggest challenge. I try to say a couple of outrageous things every class, so they will get used to stupid statements by authority figures. And teachers here are authority figures, unlike in America.

The most common suggestion, in fact it's in every student's paper, is for the politicians to provide more money, and the problem will be "all better." This is the strategy Mommy uses for every toddler booboo, a kiss to make it all better. This policy alternative is ubiquitous and proves they have learned the primary lesson from American politics. My work here is done.

Item - the USA will pay to clean up
nuclear problems in Russia.
Item - the USA will pay to fix
environmental problems in Lithuania.
Item - the USA will pay to convert
defense industries in Poland.
Item - the USA will pay to decommission
nuclear subs rotting in the ocean.
Item - the USA will pay, the USA will pay,
and the USA will pay.
Did I mention the USA would pay?

It is not surprising to hear that Poland threatens to sell tanks to Iran unless the USA would like to pay Poland NOT to sell them. It is not surprising that Ukraine has come up with a schedule to shut down Chernobyl, all the West has to do is come up with the money. It is not surprising that Russia will sell nuclear technology to Iran. Because, they say, if we don't pay, someone else will. This is yet another tactic the West is exporting.

O.K. class, it's time for another pop quiz. "Why is it O.K. for the USA to sell nuclear reactors to North Korea, but not for the Russians to sell reactors to Iran? Class?" No answer? This is what happens when you confuse profit with policy.

World War Duh

Not being able to understand the intricacies and intrigues of diplomacy and foreign policy, I call old Machiavelli up on his cell phone for a quick lesson in being the ruler of a country.

'So, Mach old buddy," I begin, "what do you think of this whole East West power trip thing? We thought that after the fall of the wall, we wouldn't have this stuff anymore."

"Hey, it's nothing new," Machiavelli said, "we had exactly the same situation here in Italia in the 15th century. We had all these princes, each got to have his own city, and nobody gets nothing done, what with the constant bickering."

"So what was your advice back then?" I queried, "What did they pay you the big bucks for?"

"Well..." Machiavelli hesitated, pondering whether he could make a couple of trillion lire on a consulting fee here. "The first thing I told them is that the only duty of those in government is to keep the power. The next thing is that the government has a different morality than common folks. Lastly, I gave them permission to deceive the public, to lie, to cheat, to do whatever it takes to stay in power."

"That did the trick?" I said. "It can't be that simple," I continued. "Any kid running for president of third grade knows all that stuff."

"No, no, no, nothing is that simple, not even cooking the spaghetti," Machiavelli corrected me.

"Well, what was it then? We have got to get off the dime here, we don't want to keep arguing all the way through the 21st century," I urged.

"O.K., O.K., it wasn't me all right? I didn't fix nothing back then, I just took credit, you happy?" Machiavelli cried.

"Jeez Louise, Mach, I don't care who gets the credit, I just want to know the secret, O.K.?" I cried myself.

"Well, if you must know," Machiavelli said, "don't tell nobody, but it was really those religious freaks from the East or wherever. All those Italian princes couldn't agree on how thick a pizza crust should be, much less something important."

"It took a real barbarian from outside Italy to get them together. They were so scared of an invasion that they couldn't even catch the pizza after they threw it up in the air." "Big deal," I sigh, "for that to work in our century, it would take an attack of aliens, real outer space monsters, for us to work together."

"Exactamundo," Machiavelli shouts, "now you got the idea.

"Where are we going to get an invasion from the stars," I mumble plaintively, "I can't call 1-900-GREENMEN."

"You don't need a real invasion, you dope, that would be too much trouble. All you need is for everybody to think you have an invasion," Machiavelli finished.

"That's an idea," I muse, "I wonder if I still have a cell number for Orson Welles?"

The best story in the local news lately is the ongoing one about the Russian Air Force. In their haste to get out of Dodge, I mean Kiev, the Russian Air Force left quite a few bomber and fighter aircraft sitting on runways in Ukraine.

Ukraine would love to have an instant Air Force, but they don't have the money to even fly the planes. Instead of giving the planes back to the Russians, Ukraine offered to sell them back for about two hundred fifty million dollars, and change.

The Russians know that Ukraine can't afford to fly the planes, so they offered a pittance (the current exchange rate for a pittance is three rubles) to get the planes back. Now Ukraine will GIVE the aircraft back, and the Russians will FORGIVE a debt of the equivalent two hundred million dollars that Ukraine owes for oil. You gotta love a country that learns capitalism so fast.

Wedding Bell Blues

Eva is getting married. Eva is an administrative assistant here at U Brat, and she is marrying a local boy, a student. They met at the "Society for the Preservation of Slovak Music and Dance," where Eva sings and dances and Paolo plays the violin and sings. O.K., Eva sings and Paolo just shouts the words along with the music. When you are trying to save country folk music, anything goes. You gotta love a country where young people get together and have some good clean fun with centuries old music and dance.

Anyway, Eva brought the invitation to me in person, so I said, "Yes, of course, I would be honored." Later, I wander around talking with people trying to find out what kind of wedding present is appropriate. My local friends agree that a present is inappropriate, that all that is required is flowers: lots of flowers, armloads of flowers, fields of flowers, boatloads of flowers. Did I mention Eva expects flowers?

Since this is a heavily Catholic country, I am interested in whether this is going to be a civil or a church ceremony. On the appointed day and time, I find that it is a civil ceremony, conducted in an old building in Old Town.

The room, on the second floor, is some kind of wedding factory. We are all standing out in the hall, milling around, like cattle before a stampede. We have that same nervous energy, and at precisely 5 pm, doors open.

The first few in get to sit on little curved couches arranged in a semicircle around a table, with the rest of us standing against the back wall. An organist provides the obligatory music, the doors open once again, and here comes the bride. Oh yeah, and the groom.

There are several speeches in Slovak I can't follow. At last, a guy playing a traditional instrument stops these longwinded friends of the bride. The instrument looks like a cross between a flute and a good-sized hollow tree. It takes two hands and both feet, as well as some kind of leather harness for the guy to hold it vertically. It must be easier to play than it looks; the guy is not sweating nearly as much as the groom.

After the musical interlude, the two exchange vows, and then more speeches. There are speeches by the civil servants, the parents, the best man, and strangers who happen by while all this is underway. By the clock, this whole thing only took about 29 minutes, but it seemed a lot longer. Security ushers us back out into the hall through a different door. As I am the last one out, I can see the next wedding party coming in behind us. The efficiency is impressive; the gene pool here must be a lot closer to Germany than to Italy.

Out in the hall, there is a reception line, and we all troop by the blushing bride and glowing groom, hand in our obligatory flowers to a waiting flower girl, and hit the street. I try to hang around to get invited to the party, which I am sure is about to happen, but it turns out to be family only.

I ask some friends how the marriage ceremony has changed since the communist days, and the somewhat surprising answer is not much. It turns out that there are relatively more civil service marriages now and fewer church ones; but the main point is that there are fewer marriages, period. It seems that now young people have more choices, and they are choosing marriage less.

CATHOLIC, SMATHOLIC

This is a Catholic country now, but it took interesting twists and turns along the way. After the Magyar Invasion of 896, the Czechs and Slovaks followed different paths.

In Bohemia, what is now the Czech Republic, there were a series of kings, most of whom seemed to have trouble leaving heirs. In-breeding does funny things. A king can get away with almost anything, but not leaving a son behind is usually fatal to the country. This is exactly why we invented vice-presidents in America.

For example, the dynasty of the Premyslids ended when the teenage Vaclav III was murdered. His father suddenly died, apparently, from eating and drinking to excess. I guess bulimia was not yet invented. Vaclav III had four sisters, but girls didn't count in Bohemia. What to do? The noblemen got together and, since they couldn't agree on a local boy, they offered the throne to a German who was married to Vaclav III's youngest sister.

This guy, named John, loved the idea since he wanted to start wars everywhere but he didn't have any money of his own. He made Bohemia cough up the dough to support the doughboys, and he went off to war with his own private army. Luckily for Bohemia, King John got himself killed in battle before he completely bankrupted the country, and his son, Charles IV, took over.

The Bohemians lucked out with Charles IV, who was substantially more intelligent than your average king, and he started a university in Prague in 1348. He was so good at this ruler stuff that he was elected Holy Roman Emperor in addition to being the King of Bohemia. Today, this would be analogous to being the Queen of England and the Pope, simultaneously.

After his death, his son Vaclav IV reverted to type and got thrown in jail regularly. This was embarrassing, even for a king, and the country went downhill rapidly. This was probably the origin of diplomatic immunity.

GOING PLACES

In today's world, one thing that Bratislava has lots of is bookstores. In fact, it seems as if most of the stores downtown are either bookstores or travel agencies. They alternate down the block. After cable TV gets here, the bookstores will probably die out.

For a country that is supposed to be suffering from the pangs of a communist economy, it is amazing to see travel agent after travel agent with posters in the windows offering the latest great deals on a new vacation site. In America, these storefronts fill up with real estate agents, but here it's travel agents. You have to wonder where the people get the money to go to Egypt, China, and all the other points of the compass that are advertised in every window. Don't ask. I don't know.

Tonight I decide to go to a movie. First, I need to find a movie poster somewhere around town to see what is playing where. It really helps that the movie posters here are not for a particular movie. They list all the movies at all the theaters in town, along with starting times. I must not be the only person who can't make a phone call.

Once you choose a movie, you figure out a combination of trams and buses that will get you there before the movie starts. At the theater comes the really fun part. When you buy a ticket, the ticket is for a particular seat, identified by row number and seat number. I can do numbers up to about ten in Slovak, but saying something like "I would like a seat on the left side, row 24, seat 13," is beyond me. I resort to hand language and pantomime, with flashbacks of kitty litter.

This works all right most of the time, the problem comes when I try to get a ticket for a seat that is not contiguous with the seats already sold. In Slovak theaters, everyone wants to sit toward the back, right in the middle of the row. Consider a theater with thirty rows of thirty seats. The first tickets sold will be row 30, seats 15 and 16. The next will be row 30, seats 13 and 14 and 17 and 18.

Then they will move to row 29 and repeat the process, with everyone sitting next to the last person to buy a ticket, or directly in front of that person. Silly me, I like to sit more toward the front and toward the side, so I don't have anyone right in front of me and I have room for my long legs.

This is a beeg problem in most theaters because they have a book of tickets printed for each performance, and when you ask for a certain ticket by row and seat, they have to thumb through the book until they find that page and, using a ruler as a guide, carefully tear out your ticket from the book. Usually they just say no. Thus, you understand the preference for selling the next ticket in the book rather than finding a new page and having to carefully tear out a ticket from the middle.

If the theater is not crowded, I simply accept the next ticket in order and then sit wherever I want. This usually works fine, however I exercise caution with this tactic as Slovaks seem to be genetically incapable of sitting in just any seat, feeling compelled to sit in the one assigned to them by the current authorities.

One of the last times a friend and I went to a theater in town, we tried to use this tactic. We accepted our tickets in the middle of one of the back rows, but when we got inside, the seats were about ninety percent empty, so we went forward a few empty rows, and picked a couple of seats at the end of the row.

After the movie started, people kept coming in (I guess the tram was late). Somehow, there had been a terrible mistake by the ticket seller, and they were selling tickets for the row we had chosen. Despite the fact that there were dozens of empty seats all around us, each new group would come in, stand there looking at their seat assignments for a long while, and then ask us to move so they could go to the middle of our row. After about the third group came in, we moved up a few rows and had no more problems.

Now, there are a couple of theaters in Bratislava that have a new computerized ticketing system. *Wow,* I think, *there won't be any more trouble getting a ticket for the seat I want.*

O.K., so I was wrong. When you get to the window to buy a ticket at these theaters, a computer screen has replaced the traditional book of tickets. The ticket seller is sitting there with a mouse driven cursor and just has to click on the seat that you point to, and the ticket is computer printed. Neat. Except you still can't get a ticket that is not right next to the last ticket sold. Don't ask. I really, really, really don't know, and I don't want to talk about it anymore.

Oh yeah, I forgot to check if this movie has subtitles. If dubbed, it is difficult for me to understand the dialogue. After I get in, it turns out that the movie is dubbed in Slovak or Czech, I can't tell which, without English subtitles. Pop quiz, class: can you get the message from a movie from just the visuals and no soundtrack? Well, yes, since the movie is *Free Willie.* The dialogue is superfluous. I don't know if I will try this with another movie or not. One that is too complex for your average chimp to follow, unlike Free Willie.

Hey, I know what you are thinking, but you try living in Eastern Europe for a year without TV or a golf course, and you will end up going to every American movie that comes along, too.

TAKE THE A TRAIN

When you get out of the theater late, it is night bus time. Night buses are a whole different ball game. People who are familiar with life in Southern California will agree that the locals there have a unique way of referring to the freeway system. Instead of saying something like:

> "I took Interstate 5 down to U.S. Highway 101, then got on State Route 19 over to Interstate 110, and stayed on it until I got to the Pacific Coast Highway,"

a resident of LA might say:
> "I grabbed the 5 down to the 101, took the 19 over to the 110 all the way to the PCH."

Here in Bratislava, we talk a little like that, except about public transportation. We might say:

> "I jumped on the 56, down to the 5, over to the 101, slipped on the 12 until O.T."

The translation is:
> "I rode the electric bus number 56 down to where I could get on tram number 5, took that to the stop where the express autobus

> 101 makes a stop, got on, and rode until I
> came to the beginning of trolley number 12,
> which I took all the way into Old Town."

See, you are learning to speak Slovak already. One trick that can be useful here in the middle of Zima, when you are waiting an hour in the dark of a freezing night rain for Bus 29, is to take the first tram that comes along to "anywhere" for about twenty minutes, until you can see another tram coming toward you. Get off, go across the street, and take the opposite tram back to your stop.

If you time it right, you get back just as Bus 29 pulls up. If you are two seconds late you get to try again, but at least you haven't frozen to death waiting. I did not invent this tactic, and some nights I join a small group of freezing Slovaks attempting this life-saving maneuver.

Dashing Through The Snow

The first week in December, up go the lights and other Christmas decorations. Old Town has lights strung all over, green, blue, yellow, and red. Only the red ones seem to blink. There are portable shops up in all the squares selling all manner of local handcrafts. Food carts are everywhere in between the shops selling something hot: hot wine, hot dogs, hot peppers, hot goulash, hot treats from all over.

This all looks suspiciously like Christmas in some parts of the USA until you see your first tub of water containing humongous carp. Carp, you know, the fish. Suddenly, there are tubs of live carp everywhere. There are carp tubs in front of the stands, carp tubs behind the stands, carp tubs under the stands, and carp tubs in the middle of the street.

I am spending the holidays with my friend Patricia and her family, so I ask "what is it with all these carp?"

Small Slovakian girl
wrestling traditional carp
home for Christmas dinner.

"Carp is the traditional dish served," Patricia patiently explains, "at Christmas dinner."

"Oh," I said. "How about doing something different, like a nice Chinese restaurant?"

"Oh no," Patricia insists, "we always have a Christmas carp, and we will this year."

"Naturally," I said, "but how does the carp get from swimming around happily in the tub to the dinner table?"

"We pick out the one we want and hit it over the head with a wooden mallet," she said, "and put it in the freezer until Christmas."

Later, I hear that some people have another tradition. They take the carp home in a big baggie, like you used to do with goldfish when you were a kid, and let it swim around in the bathtub until mallet time. You should see the smile on kid's faces when they see the carp heading for a three-week bath.

Here people give each other a small, usually handmade gift, and don't try to blame the size or color or bad taste on Saint Nick.

Christmas morning finally comes to this small village in eastern Slovakia. I was hoping for a white Christmas, since it is certainly cold enough and I don't get to see all that much snow in Florida, but no luck.

I wake up in anticipation of unwrapping presents under the tree. But no, you aren't allowed to unwrap your present on Christmas morning, that pleasure is saved until evening.

The men will spend the day taking walks in the winter woods. The women will cook the special Christmas carp, special Christmas salad, special Christmas potatoes, and special Christmas cake. Some things never change. You gotta love a country where the guys don't even have to help with the dishes.

9

Too Good To Be True

"It was worse than a crime, it was a blunder."
Tallyrand, on Napoleon's
killing of duc d'Enghien

The New Year means new classes at Slovak U, as well as the continuation of the other class at U Brat. January is devoted to oral exams, by those who give oral exams (not me). That means the new term does not start until sometime in February or March, depending on I know not what.

Later during this term, which is scheduled to go until June 1, the chairman came to me and said; "we're changing the schedule. Now, all of your classes will end a month earlier on May 1."

"I have scheduled lectures through June 1," I said, "do you suggest I talk faster, or just cut out stuff?"

Before I finished the sentence, he was gone. Now I had the task of fitting in all the material in fewer classes. No beeg problem, until the chairman came to me again and said, "We changed the schedule again, now your classes will end April 15." I figured I was making progress; they only cut two weeks this time.

Slovak U is old, older than the hills, some say. Here there are stacks of professors, resembling so much dead wood. I guess the tenure system is strangling higher education here, just as in the USA. My class will be undergraduates in the department of political science, and since this is not a required class, they can choose to come or not. Some come just to take a gander at an American class.

The night before the first day of class, I have a nightmare. Suppose I gave a course and no one came. There I am standing in front of an empty room, lecturing to empty chairs. This is the opposite of U Brat, where they have students but no professors. The morning brings relief, as six students actually show up. Really eight, if you count the two Slovak lecturers from the department who were "required" to appear by the dean. Thank you, dean.

The lecture is not too painful. The students actually ask more questions than they did at U Brat. This is more of a real university than U Brat, which is kind of a professional training school. Here the students seem to be more inquisitive, more open to new ideas. At U Brat, the students are there to get a degree, with the obligatory official stamp, of course, which will get them a job.

The idea of new ideas is a new idea, here in this ex-communist country. For the last seventy years or so, new ideas in Soviet Bloc countries have met with the same level of enthusiasm that would greet the Pope if he had an original thought.

"Come on you cardinals," the Pope might say, "let's tell all the Catholics that they can cut out the middleman and talk directly to God, like the Baptists. After all, I talk directly to God, so maybe I'm a Baptist." The cardinals would have a collective heart attack. It could happen.

This building has been in continuous use
as an Apothecary since before Columbus.
There are never any apartments for rent.

THE GREAT SCHISM

One of the most interesting times in the history of the Catholic Church in Europe was the era of dueling popes. There was one pope in Rome, of course, but a pope wannabe set up shop in Avignon, unable to wait until the death of the real pope for his shot at the title.

Kind of like the World Boxing Association and the International Boxing Federation having different heavy weight titleholders at the same time. Who is the real champ? They didn't settle the dispute in the ring by the Marquis of Queensbury rules. The dueling popes didn't even have a dual. They started a war, showing that same lack of originality all religions carry like a cross.

These so-called inter-papal wars were eating into church profits, as they tried to develop the first true "star wars" weapons, using divine intervention and real stars. To fill the war chests, both pope pretenders claim they got approval from God to sell religious indulgences to finance their armies of mercenaries. Or armies of true believers, depending on which version you believe.

A religious indulgence is kind of like those $5000 a plate dinners that the Republicans are always throwing. If you buy enough of them, you get to be the ambassador to some third world country.

Except with a religious indulgence you get to commit some sin with impunity. Wait a minute, an ambassador gets to sin with impunity too; we just call it "sinning with immunity." The richer you are, the more commandments you get to break. Is this a great religion, or what? Actually, this is a good example of what the comic strip character Pogo used to call "the golden rule." Whoever has the gold, makes the rules.

This was developing into a problem all over Europe, but in Bohemia, a peasant born preacher named Jan Hus decided that enough was enough, and he wasn't going to take it anymore. Hus started preaching all this heresy to the masses, getting them all riled up. The king de jour, Vaclav IV, backed Hus for personal reasons. O.K., Hus was actually the confessor to the Queen, and with her support, Hus really got rolling.

A couple of years later, things were getting out of hand. King Vaclav IV was back in prison, this time put there by his brother, and unable to defend Hus. Hus was making things too hot for the church and the state, so they declared, "you are a heretic, and you are gonna burn at the stake." This meant martyrdom for Hus, and thus Hus began the Hussite Wars.

It also set the stage for another Vaclav, Vaclav Havel, who was jailed many times over the years from 1969 until 1989, for inciting the people to protest against the state. Of course, this time the state was the communist state instead of the Catholic Church, but the basic idea is the same. He also set the stage and raised the curtain for the velvet revolution. This is what happens when you confuse politics with religion.

School Daze

The whole idea of what we call school today, developed by the guy called the father of the modern school, was to teach everyone to read so that they could study the bible on their own. The Catholic Counter Reformation drove this guy, a Czech named Comenius, out of this area in the 17th century. He couldn't fight the Catholics with force anymore, so he developed the idea of universal literacy as a way of making it possible to remain a Protestant, without the bother of a church.

In addition, he invented the "primer," what we call textbooks today, and developed a whole new curriculum for education. My students are not too thrilled when I tell them that a Czech was responsible for their misery.

WINDOWS 95

Before he burned, Hus started attacking the sale of religious indulgences, Vaclav did a quick flip-flop after realizing he was losing profits. Some American presidents later reintroduced the flip-flop.

This flip-flop so enraged the Hussites that they grabbed some nearby Catholic priests and threw them through a window on an upper floor of a downtown Prague office building. Kind of like stockbrokers after the 1929 crash, however these guys didn't jump of their own free will.

This little episode was Prague's First Defenestration. The word "fenster" means window in German, so you get the idea. And you are right, there was a second one, but not for a couple of hundred years. The Hussites split into two factions, the radicals who went in for defenestration, and the moderates who were afraid of heights. Although

A Slovak nun strolls through Old Town,
resisting the temptation to buy something.

they hung around for a while, this was all she wrote for the Hussites.

MORE KINGS

The next few hundred years are known as the "dark ages" to the Czechs, who somehow got stuck with those genetic wonders, the Hapsburgs, after the Turks stole most of Hungary. They let them keep what was euphemistically called "Upper Hungary," which was actually Slovakia, north of the Danube River. Since Hungary was MIA, the current Hapsburgs had nothing much to do, since there isn't much call for out of work kings. This is exactly why we limit presidents to two terms.

During this time, the war between the Protestants and the Catholics was waged back and forth with first the king in this country favoring this religion and then the king in that country favoring that religion. In the early 1600's, a few more Catholic nobles were defenestrated. The windows of Prague castle the chosen site this time.

I guess the Catholics were lucky that this didn't become an annual fund raising event. The disciples of Defenestration bring to mind the classic definition of a fanatic as "someone, who, having lost sight of his original aim, redoubles his efforts."

The remaining Catholics got so annoyed they redoubled their efforts. They persecuted Protestants, they burned Protestants at the stake, and they killed Protestants. Even worse, they invited Jesuit missionaries to come in and set up shop. All forms of Protestantism got an "X" rating and the education system fell into the hands of those wild and crazy guys, the Jesuits.

You remember the characters on the original Saturday Night Live show played by Steve Martin and Dan Akroyd, the "wild and crazy guys?" Well, those characters were Czechoslovakian, but even they weren't Jesuits.

While the Czechs had all this stuff up with which to put, the Slovaks were even worse off, if possible. They spent almost a thousand years as the northern outpost of the Hungarian Kingdom. They remained rural, and positively feudal. The Hapsburgs, having nothing better to do, temporarily took the reins of Hungary, but no matter who was in charge, there was never any thought of autonomy for the Slovaks.

From a Slovakian viewpoint, the difference between Budapest and Vienna being in charge was a moot point, so the 1867 Dual Monarchy of Austria-Hungary was just more of the same, not unlike the Double Mint Twins. After this, the forced Magyarization of Slovakia increased to the point where, by 1914, twenty percent of the Slovak population had emigrated, most of them to the USA.

Genetics Rules

Call the Nobel Prize committee, and show me the money. I have developed incontrovertible proof that there is a significant physiological difference between men and women. It is abundantly obvious that males produce ten times as much spit as women.

Here in Slovakia, man and boy spit on the average of twenty times a minute: once every three seconds. Walking down the sidewalk, the biggest obstacle is not avoiding people and it is not missing the potholes. It is not even dodging the open manholes. It is eluding the gobs of spittle every two feet.

I have seen young men in their prime up the spit rate to once every second, but even the most masculine teenage Neanderthal can't keep up that rate for more than one minute. This is genetically encoded, since Slovak women never spit.

Did you hear the one about the West German who visited East Germany shortly after the fall of the wall?

He was walking down the street with a potential business colleague, when he suddenly stopped, unzipped his pants, and relieved himself on the street corner. The East German looked at him incredulously and said, "What are you doing? There is no toilet here." The West German looked slowly first one way down the street, and then the other, before replying "There should be."

Speaking of West Germans, while you occasionally see a BMW or Mercedes here, the prevalent car is a relatively nice, relatively cheap Skoda. This name translates as (I swear on a stack of policy textbooks), "it's a pity." In that case, the monumentally miserable East German car, the "Trabent" must translate as, "it's a crime."

KEEPERS OF THE GATE

"What happened," I am always asking people here, "to all the guys who used to be in charge, the communists? Where are they today? Where did they go? Before the velvet revolution communists were everywhere, they were running everything; they were totally in control."

Actually, no one will admit to being a communist now, everyone running for office claims to have been a dissident. I think that being a dissident in the old days was like Jimmy Carter committing adultery in his heart. Who knew?

Since no one will fess up to being an ex-communist, I have developed my own theory. My theory is that under the communist regime, there were tons of people that I call "gatekeepers." These were the people who were responsible for one little flow in the bureaucracy.

One little section of rubles, or goods, or services was their sole bailiwick. They collected something, they charged for something, or they stamped something. As the communist state started withering, they kept doing their thing, but now nobody was watching. Instead of passing the goodies up the line, they "diverted" whatever they controlled.

First, they diverted a little stuff. Then some more stuff, and then a lot of stuff. Finally, there was a magical time when the communists were history, but no one else was replacing them yet. During this period, the gatekeepers could sock away everything that passed through their gate. They suddenly learned the errors of their old communist ways, and they simultaneously learned the virtues of being a capitalist. Those numbered accounts the Swiss invented for the Nazis really started to pay off.

All I know is that just after the revolution, when you could actually buy something; like a house, a business, or a car some people had lots of money. You could see a guy living in a brand new big house on the hill, driving a brand new blue BMW, talking on his brand new cell phone. When you ask, "who is that guy?" the answer is "he used to be in charge of some gate." This is what happens when you confuse communism with capitalism.

Every law student in the USA gets a similar lecture sometime during his education. This is the talk where the old lawyer explains the economic facts of life to the young lawyer. He tells the budding jurist that "in every transaction, there is a magic moment where the money has left the hands of the party of the first part, but has not yet arrived into the hands of the party of the second part. This is the moment, my son," the old lawyer triumphantly cackles, "when you get yours."

10

Life And Death

"The problem with communication is the assumption it has been accomplished."
George Bernard Shaw

Gabriela was buried this afternoon. Gabriela was the best and the brightest. She was the smartest student in my class last term at U Brat, the one who won all the awards. The one voted most likely to succeed, the one with the best English, the one with the most friendly, outgoing personality. The valedictorian, head cheerleader, and prom queen all rolled into one vibrant package. Everyone loved Gabby.

Last term, when I was looking for a new place to live, I asked my class to be on the lookout for an apartment within my price range. It turned out that almost every student in the class was looking for an apartment also, since most had no choice but to live with their parents. Including Gabby. Gabby and her boyfriend, a tall, good-looking guy who worked upstairs at IBM, seemed like the perfect young couple. They had drive, intelligence, ambition, and talent. Unlike most students, they also had money, thanks to IBM.

Gabby and I talked on several occasions about our mutual search for a place to live, sharing leads that never seemed to work out. This is why young couples live with parents. One day I got a chance to look at a small efficiency apartment that had been vacant for several years. This vacancy is not all that unusual, many flats are controlled by someone who doesn't live there, but can't legally rent it, so it's empty. Don't ask. I don't know.

This particular flat is tempting, but not exactly what I am looking for. It's about halfway up one of the ubiquitous communist panelaks, and I have my heart set on a little stone cottage. So I tell Gabby about the place, and give her the phone number of the person who controls it. He doesn't care about renting it illegally, because he doesn't need a receipt.

"It is perfectna," Gabby excitedly told me. "My boyfriend and I will finally have our own home, and now we can get married," she finished.

After the holidays, when class was starting again, Gabby was conspicuous by her absence. This didn't make any sense. She had been in the program for a year and a half years and was almost finished. All she talked about was getting the degree, and getting a job. Other class members were equally confused, saying that she had not been in any of their other classes.

After the second week of class, when she was still missing, some friends became concerned to the point that they went over to the flat I had recommended, looking for her. Still not finding any evidence of where or how she had disappeared, they finally decided to call the police, usually avoided at all costs in eastern Europe. The police broke into the apartment and found Gabby and her boyfriend.

They had been dead more than two weeks. The police said it was an accident, the result of a faulty gas heater.

Hundreds of family and friends of the promising young people attended the funeral, on a cold sunny afternoon the second week in February. There was music, and flowers, and an endless line of friends remembering the young lovers. Not being able to understand any words, I knew exactly what they meant. This was an incomprehensible tragedy for Gabby, her family, and her friends.

As tragic as her death was, sometimes I couldn't help but dwell on the fact that if I had not given her the housing tip, she might still be alive. In that case, it might have been me living in that flat, with that gas heater.

What I couldn't understand, however, was the reaction of the administration at U Brat. I was the only member of the faculty and staff to attend the funeral. Whenever I would bring Gabby up in a conversation, I always got exactly the same response, "it was just an accident, and besides, she didn't suffer, she died in her sleep." Everyone who didn't go to her service repeats this statement to me at least twenty times in the next two weeks. I always knew that if it had happened to someone else, Gabby would have had more to say than that inadequate rationalization. We miss you Gabriela, we really, really, really miss you.

WHICH ONE HAS THE TONI?

On the bus home this afternoon, I sit across from the same two guys I always seem to sit across from on our way home to the quaint little village of Devin. These two guys do some kind of manual labor, since they take the early morning bus into Bratislava, wearing identical clean overalls and steel toed work boots, and carrying a brown bag that has "lunch" written all over it. In the evening, their overalls are not so clean, and the brown bags are empty.

What makes them interesting is that they look so much alike. For months, I thought they were brothers, maybe even twins. They both look old enough to be fathers, maybe even grandfathers. Both have a neatly trimmed mustache and beard, and they both wear thick glasses. They both sit impassively staring straight ahead during the twenty-minute bus ride. They get off at the same stop and walk slowly up the hill.

It was months before I found out, quite by accident, that they are actually father and son. To this day, I can't tell which is which. My only theory is that the son is one of those guys who were born old. You know the type, the kid who is always serious, and the child who never plays or fools around. The one who gets a job while still in school, and works every day for the rest of his life.

My attention is diverted from these two guys, for a while, by a little canine melodrama. An elderly lady rides the bus regularly, carrying a fake Adidas gym bag with her at all times. This is not unusual enough to notice, it seems most people on the bus carry a gym bag, but this time she puts the bag on the floor of the bus at her feet, instead of on her lap. Most people keep their hands on their stuff while on the bus. At the next stop, a young man gets on the bus along with his German shepherd, wearing the required muzzle.

After the bus starts moving, the gym bag seems to move. Maybe it is my imagination. A few seconds later, it moves again. About this time, a doll-sized dog head wiggles its way up out of the gym bag. When the gym bag dog sees the real German shepherd, it ducks quickly out of sight.

A few seconds later, it sneaks a peek again. This time the shepherd isn't looking, so the gym bag dog looks him over. When the shepherd slowly swings his massive head around, the gym bag dog ducks back into the safety of

Adidas Land. As the shepherd loses interest and looks away, here comes the head again, poking out. This game is played for several stops, entertaining us all. Hey, any old diversion is welcome on a long bus ride.

Speaking of diversions, just one more dog story. Last week I was standing at the bus stop. I would say that I was waiting for a bus, but you knew that. It wasn't raining then, but it had been and there were puddles everywhere. I was standing there, the bus was late, and along came a guy walking down the other side of the street with his little mongrel type dog. About the size of a full-grown cat, except it was a dog. The dog was trotting along in the street happily splashing through the puddles, just like any two-year-old toddler.

As the dog got across from me, he saw a particularly nice puddle and headed directly across the middle of it. When he got to about the middle of the puddle, he dropped out of sight. Completely. The puddle was actually a small lake where some workmen has been working, and had left a hole about two feet deep. Filled up with rainwater, it looked just like every other puddle.

GOLDILOCKS SYNDROME

An acquaintance of mine, a Czech citizen who has been living in a nice little flat in Prague for the last few years, has an offer of a good job in Bratislava. She decides to take the job, but then faces the same dilemma we all face here, finding a flat to rent. Since she speaks the language and has friends here, she thinks that it will not be such a beeg problem.

For several weekends, she takes the train down and goes flat hunting. This turns out to be much harder than she thought, but finally she gets a line on a furnished place that is controlled by an associate of a friend of a colleague of a neighbor of her cousin. Or something like that.

Since the location is good, the furniture is nice, and the price is right, she takes it and moves in the following Monday morning. The entire next week she is happily getting settled in her new job and her new home.

On Friday, she and her boyfriend go out to dinner to celebrate. When they arrive home at about midnight, they are shocked to discover a strange man asleep in their bed. Thinking they are the latest victims of a serial sleeper, they have just started to call the police when the guy wakes up.

After what I gather was an interesting and lengthy conversation, they discover that the flat actually belongs to this guy. Since he works out of the city all week, he asked his cousin to rent it out just during the week. He planned to use it on the weekends. Really folks, I don't make this stuff up. I couldn't make this stuff up.

Snow No Mo

It is finally March 21, the first day of spring, the day I have been eagerly anticipating all winter. Too bad there is a cold north wind, and a drizzling rain that changes to snowflakes by early afternoon. Snow does not accumulate on the ground, and it is possible that I imagined the whole episode. All traces have disappeared by the next morning, but the cold rain is back. By early afternoon, so are the snowflakes. Once again, it is gone with the morning light. De javu all over again.

Maybe this is the spring pattern: rain in the morning, snow in the afternoon, and everything disappears at night. You think you are hallucinating. For the next few weeks, from the first day of spring until Easter Sunday, we have the same freezing repetition.

The snow that falls down in the afternoon seems to fall up again while we are sleeping. My Slovak friends try to console me, the guy from Florida, wandering around carrying his tennis racquet like a security blanket to keep warm. They all have the same monotonous mantra, "Oh, this is so unusual, we NEVER have snow this time of year."

"Right," I mutter coldly, "this must be the snow from hell."

CRIME MAY PAY

Three friends and I have cabin fever. Before we, like Jimmy Buffet, shoot six holes in our freezer, we decide to take the night train to Krakow, for a little serious touristing. After work one Friday, we load up our backpacks and head for the train station. Getting off Tram #1 at the station, we see what looks to us like a family of Romanies to our untrained eye, giving us the eye. Now don't write me a bunch of letters, I know this is a cliché, but hey, there they were.

As we head up the stairs to buy tickets, the family of Romanies makes sort of a circle around us, moving along with us. We aren't too concerned, first because Romanies are everywhere here, second it is still daylight, and third there are hordes of people around.

Just before we get to the entrance to the bus station, a fight breaks out just in front of us. This appears to be a serious fight, between two young Romany men, with lots of shouting, and shoving, and swearing. We don't really care about family squabbles, but they are right in the doorway, and we can't get by.

We are watching the fight and waiting to get through the door, when suddenly my friend Steve's wife, Shirley, starts screaming at the top of her lungs. She is jumping up and down, hollering, and pointing at the Romanies behind us, shouting that one of them is trying to pick her husband's pocket. Steve reaches for his wallet, but it's already a goner.

Winter in Slovakia. It looks just like Aspen
would look, if all the SUV's were stolen.

As we realize we have been the victims of an elaborately
staged scam, we all start bellowing. The Slovaks within
earshot come to our defense and close in a ring around
the Romany family so they can't make a getaway. By now,
everyone is screaming and pointing at everyone else: some
accusing in English, some screaming along in Slovak, and
some defending in Romany.

Someone yells that the "poleizi" are on the way, and
at about this time the wallet reappears. It just floats out
of the crowd in slow motion, landing on the ground at
our feet. Of course, no one actually sees who coughed it
up, but the money, passport, and stuff are still there. The
police come quickly, but with "no harm, no foul," there is
nothing that can be done. We decide to get on the train,
showing a little more caution.

The train heads northeast through the mountains
toward Poland, and we gradually calm down a little bit
as the adrenaline wears off. We all decide that this will
make a good story for the book we each say we are going
to write some day, maybe.

Sometime after midnight, just as we are trying to doze
off, the train makes a stop. The station is on the left side

of the car, but our compartment is on the right, so we are facing out into the woods. Suddenly four men come out of the trees, approach the train from the wrong side, and get on the train several cars down from us.

After our experience at the train station, we are all more than a little paranoid. As the train starts moving again, we find the conductor and tell him about the four guys. His answer is, "I am not a policeman, and there is nothing I can do until the next stop. Anyway," he continues, "they are probably hiding and will jump off before we can get the police."

We decide we are just nervous for nothing, but we decide to close the door to our compartment and tie it shut with our belts, so that no one can open the door while we are sleeping.

A couple of hours later, you guessed it, Shirley starts screaming again. As the rest of us struggle to figure out what is going on, we see the four guys in the corridor trying to get into our compartment. Since they can't get the door open, they have removed a piece of glass from a windowpane beside the door and are trying to get to our belts holding the door closed.

We all start yelling, and they beat a retreat. This is what happens when you confuse discretion with valor. Finding the sleeping conductor again, he tells us, you guessed it, "There is nothing I can do until the next stop."

None of us get any more sleep that night waiting for the next stop. Finally, the train rolls into a little town just before the Polish border and we crowd around the compartment window watching to see if the conductor makes a dash for the cops. What a surprise, he is nowhere to be seen. Instead, we see our four new friends strolling along the platform, as if they were on their way to church. As they pass our compartment, one tips his hat in our direction with a hint of a smile.

Later we learn that we were lucky. The most effective technique used by these guys in Eastern Europe, especially in Romania, is to wait until everyone is sleeping, then pump each compartment in the car full of some kind of gas that puts everybody to sleep. Then they can take all the time they want, as well as all of your stuff.

GO DIRECTLY TO JAIL

All this crime and no punishment is getting to me. It is getting to almost everyone, evidently, quite literally. Since the fall of the wall, all sort of regular crime increased about a jillion percent in Eastern Europe. In addition, the newspapers are full of stories about how organized crime is taking over the former USSR and the rest of Eastern Europe. Western crime such as drugs, protection rackets, counterfeiting and embezzlement are flourishing along with more traditional favorites such as prostitution and murder for hire.

Some argue that America and the West are exporting these crimes. My rebuttal is that since we still have them, we can't have exported them. Obviously, I can't figure out what is causing all this crime, much less what to do about it, so I call up old Sherlock Holmes on his cell phone to pick his brain.

"So, Sherlock," I said, "is a criminal born or made?"

"Whoa there, I don't give interviews," Sherlock said, "You better call Dr. Watson."

"Uh, well, this isn't an interview," I said, resorting to an old interviewing trick, "I just want to ask you a question."

"In that case," Sherlock announces graciously, "what is the subject of the inquiry again?"

"Right," I quickly press on, "there seems to be a lot more crime in the world today, and I wondered if some people are just born to a life of villainy, or if they learn to be criminals in school, or by watching television, or eating Twinkies?"

"Good question, old chap," Sherlock agrees, "and the answer is simple. It's as obvious as the nose on your face, if it were a snake it would bite you, if it were a woman of the evening..."

"O.K. all ready, just tell me," I plead.

"It is not necessary to be rude young man," Sherlock laments, "you Americans are always in a hurry, you want instant answers, you can't take the time to consider the question from all angles, you demand to..."

"Yeah, yeah," I agree, "do you know, or don't you?"

"Certainly I know," Sherlock said, "it is the old question of nature vs. nurture, of heredity vs. environment, of blue blood vs. bad blood...oh yes, you just want, how do you say, a quick fix. All right, the answer is yes."

"Whadda ya mean yes? Yes, criminals are born, or yes criminals are made?" I said.

"I mean yes, some people are born to crime, and yes some people have crime thrust upon them," Sherlock explains patiently, as if to a small child.

"Wait a sec," I said, "I think I get it, some people are victims of circumstance, and some choose to be outlaws, right?"

"Not exactly, old chum," Sherlock said, "but probably as close as you will come, in my lifetime."

"Well, forget that," I said, "it doesn't really matter anyway. Now that we have all these criminals, the question is, what can we do about it? Got an answer for that one, hotshot?"

"I believe I have," Sherlock replies.

"Well, spill it," I said, "I'm holding my breath."

"It's the barristers," Sherlock said.

"Whadda mean," I said, "those rails you hold onto going down the stairs?"

"No, not banisters you dolt," Sherlock almost shouted, "barristers, attorneys, lawyers."

"Wait just a golderned minute," I said, "you're telling me that it's LAWYERS that cause the crime problem?"

"But of course," said Sherlock, "in my day, when I solved a crime, and identified the perpetrator, we locked the bugger up and he stayed there." Sherlock paused for dramatic effect, "in your country, when the police arrest the culprit, his lawyer has him back on the street in about five minutes, eager to have another go. Moreover, your criminals never actually go to trial because of all the plea-bargaining. Finally, if a criminal type does have the bad luck to get tried, they get off on some technicality, thanks to their barrister."

"Is that your final answer," I said, "just shoot all the lawyers?"

"Oh no, nothing so melodramatic is required," Sherlock said, "just shut down all the law schools, and the problem will eventually disappear."

"Just how will closing the law schools reduce crime, wise guy?" I said.

"Elementary, my dear Watson," Sherlock finished, "you chaps graduate so many barristers every year that there are just not enough criminals to go around, so more and more people turn to a life of crime to keep all of the lawyers employed."

"Thanks, Sherlock," I said, "next I suppose you will be telling me that electing politicians causes the budget deficit."

SPRING GREEN

It is the first day of May, and spring is finally here for real. Just in time, too, because today a real maypole somehow magically appeared in the tiny square in the center of the quaint little village of Devin.

An Ode to Green

It is the first day of May.
Hills are green with new grass,
trees are green with new leaves.

It is that impossibly deep,
impossibly rich,
impossibly green, green.

The green of fertile soil,
pure rainwater,
golden sunshine.

Artists and poets
labor vainly to capture
this green on canvas and paper.

This green persuades you
God's in his heaven and
all's right with the world.

This green renews
the earth and the soul:
currency of the next generation.

This green makes money pale,
and green with envy.
You've seen the green I mean.

I fantasize about a maypole dance with young naked virgins dancing around in a circle holding gaily-colored ribbons, but no luck. If Eastern Europe were serious about boosting tourism, this would seriously help.

Mayday is a big deal in the communist world. It has come to represent the day of the worker, the triumph of the proletariat over the bourgeois, the victory of communism over capitalism, the mastery of common man over the dark nature of evil. If you believe that, I have some swampland in Siberia to sell.

GARDEN PARTY

Everyone in Bratislava has a summer home. Actually, what everyone has here is more of a weekend home. Since about ninety percent of the people live in tiny high-rise

Romanies on the prowl
through Stare Mesto.
Oops, just average tourists, never mind.

panelaks, these former agrarian people had to come up with a new way to get back to the land.

The solution is a garden out beyond the edge of town. The entire city of Bratislava is ringed by small, neatly divided, fenced gardens. It is the equivalent of what the wealthier inhabitants of New York City do; those who escape to their vine covered cottage up in the Hudson River Valley on weekends and during the summer heat.

Here people live in a communist paradise modeled on a Skinner Box, where behavior modification is the favorite pastime. They ride the tram out to their own 10' x 10' piece of earth. O.K. so the gardens are bigger than the 10' x 10' plot, actually the cottages are about 10' x 10' and the gardens vary from about 10' x 20' to 10' x 50' or more.

You can picture these linear plots running from the road up the side of a hill, with the tiny cabin perched at the top. The weekend cottages look sort of like a camping shelter along the Appalachian Trail. Each garden is neatly tended, with grapevines (everyone makes their own wine), flowers (everyone gives everyone flowers), fruit trees (everyone eats their own fruit), and vegetables (everyone grows vegetables, but you never see them being eaten).

Bus Stop

Coming back from your garden at the edge of town, you get to experience the "night bus." The night buses here in Bratislava are a real trip. The buses during the day are the same buses, but you get a whole different feeling at night.

At night, every bus gathers at the downtown train station parking lot at the same time. Like where the elephants go to die. Then, at precisely 11:50 p.m., they all head out at once, each bus in a different direction. Picture a hive of giant bees taking off to scout for food.

They each have their own route, and each route is timed to get the bus back down to the train station at precisely 12:50 a.m. The buses rest up and head out again, at 1:05 am.

Come along with me on a typical night bus trip. We are out in Dubravka at a friend's panelak for a party. At 12:27 a.m., we flag bus number 504 down. Unlike day buses, night buses don't stop automatically, they only stop if you can successfully get the drivers attention, and the driver is in a good mood. We make the trip to the train station, where the parking lot is full of buses waiting patiently until the next night run, and passengers waiting not so patiently for the next night run. These are mostly young, mostly drunk young men, and mostly young, mostly excited young women, heading to the next party.

Here, it is already a party: people yelling, drinking, and cursing. Everyone thinks they are being clever, funny, and sexy. The rendezvous used to be downtown Old Town at the square, but the place got so wild and crazy every night, the police moved it out to the train station.

Tonight, as most nights, we are the only passengers on night bus number 502 going out to the quaint little village of Devin. We sit all the way in the back, up high over the warm motor. In our fantasy, we are Napoleon and Josephine, being driven in our private coach up the Danube River to our castle Devin.

The driver does not stop; we glide through the night along the Danube. The six white horses trot rhythmically, the blue river flows harmoniously, and we journey dreamily.

We finally push the little white button that signals the driver that we must get off, and our private transportation glides to a halt. We step off the bus into the reality of a cold wind, and a short walk to our cottage just outside the gate to the castle. It was fun while it lasted.

11

Home Again, Home Again

"I am from nowhere."
- Andy Warhol
Actually, Andy's parents
emigrated to America
from Slovakia.

S ince the soldiers, the popes, and the megalomaniacs have failed to unify Europe, now here come "the suits." You know the suits. The suits are those people (mostly men) who come out of the executive suites in expensive suits, walk around in groups, chattering animatedly among themselves. They point in all directions, like Japanese tourists in America, but without the obligatory Nikons hanging from their necks.

You can see the evidence of this not only in the growing presence of the European Union, but also in joint ventures like the Airbus, a project that is so successful that Boeing has stopped laughing at them, and started copying them. Eventually, Europe may be unified, but in the meantime, it is a lot more fun. A McDonalds is jejune in every language. Of course, Eastern European countries eventually join the EU, and learn to use the Euro dollar, like all the other homogenized European countries. Go east now, young man, go east now.

Look For The Union Label

You can't swing a dead cat in Eastern Europe without hitting a castle. Most of these rocky ruins, built on high ground, guard a river trade route. However, every once in a while you come across a castle up on top of a hill, out in the middle of nowhere, apparently guarding nothing. This puzzled me for months.

One night while dreaming, I developed a theory that I want to try out on you. Take my castle, Castle Devin, for example. Construction began on top of a huge rock that just happens to be standing at the confluence of two important rivers. Not only that, but there were tons of rocks to build the castle, walls, and other fortifications just lying around to be picked up.

I think this last point is the key. Imagine that you are a King, Prince, or Somebody Else back in the Middle Ages. You want to build a brand spanking new castle for your brand spanking new bride (I know what you are thinking). O.K., you find a likely location, you sign a contract with the general castle contractor, and bingo, generations later you move in.

First, you are careful to choose a strategic location. It is on a hill guarding an important river, and there isn't already a castle there. If there is an existing castle on your chosen spot, you have a whole different set of problems. So far, so good.

You hire a new controversial architect, Frank Lloyd Wrightovsky, and he comes up with a daring new castle design. The cannon emplacements will cantilever out over the river. No boats, not even an Eskimo in a kayak, will be able to get past you without paying the toll. During the contract negotiations, the general castle contractor comes to you saying, "We have a beeg problem."

"What is it this time," you say, "the architect wants to add more towers, or more turrets, or what?"

"Nothing that simple," is the answer, "I have been out counting rocks. There are just not enough stones here on the site you chose to build a castle, even if we downsize the dungeon."

"So what," you say, "the stone masons can go get more rocks from that mountain at the other end of the valley, can't they?"

"No way," he says, "the stone masons union will only allow the stone masons to lay stone, not go get stone."

"So what?" you repeat, "The stone movers can move it, can't they? The stone movers union contract doesn't prevent stone movers from moving stone, does it?"

"No," he is forced to admit, "but the stone movers union has been on strike since, well, since the beginning of the Stone Age."

"What is the answer?" you demand, "what am I supposed to do now?"

"The only thing you can do," he finishes, "is build the castle down at the other end of the valley on top of that hill, in the middle of nowhere, guarding nothing. Where there are lots of rocks."

Big War

Since the beginning of time, the Czechs and Slovaks had differing histories. The idea of a Czech and Slovak union sort of formed by accident at the beginning of World War I. Lots of countries get formed by accident. Here, few men from either country were too excited about fighting side-by-side with Austrians or Hungarians, both of whom had spent years abusing the both the Czechs and the Slovaks.

Throngs of guys from both countries defected, and headed east to form the Czechoslovak Legion. They fought on the Eastern Front side-by-side with those other Slavs: Russians and Serbs. After the war, the Czechoslovak Legion ended up in Siberia, somehow involved in the Russian revolution. Don't ask. I don't know.

Meanwhile, the charismatic Czech leader, Tomas Masaryk, was in the USA campaigning for an independent Czech and Slovak state. His idea was to put together a coalition and get out from under a future dominated, yet again, by the Austro-Hungarians. This radical idea, in tune with the Allies new-found desire to break up the power and influence of the old rulers, took off. After the Great War, the new nation of Czechoslovakia began life, with a dowry of industry left over from the old regimes.

That was the good news. The bad news was that the new nation consisted of six million Czechs and two million Slovaks. Not counting three million Germans who had been slowly infiltrating Czech lands over the years. Don't forget the almost one million Hungarians who had been cut off from their own country when the Northern border of Hungary was instantly relocated south along the Danube River, thus making them instant Slovaks.

Now the jackboots were on the other feet, and it was the Czechs turn to beat up on the Germans, and the Slovaks turn to hammer on the Hungarians. This tally, of course, doesn't count the Romanies, but that's another story.

During the 1920's, when Masaryk was able to push through some badly needed reforms, such as universal suffrage and the Language Law, consensus was the order of the day. The coalition of "The Five" parties used the

catchy slogan "we have agreed that we will agree," (kind
of like a republican congress in the USA). The "Language
Law" required bilingualism in any area where the minority
was at least twenty percent. If you were a Hungarian, or
even worse, a Romanie, in an area of only nineteen percent
Hungarians or Romanies, you had to fend for yourself.

Not everyone agrees that bilingualism is a good thing.
A Colombian Bara Indian, when asked by a linguist why
there were so many languages, explained, "if we were all
Tukano speakers, where would we get our women?"

Seconds

Of these minorities, the biggest immediate problem
was the Germans, at least those living along the borders
of Bohemia and Moravia. These so-called "Sudeten
Germans" had always wanted to steal the Bohemian and
Moravian lands they lived on, but Hitler's annexation of
Austria finally gave them the perfect excuse.

Still, nothing may have happened until Prime
Minister Chamberlain of England, and his counterpart
in France, signed the Munich Diktat agreeing to ALL of
Hitler's demands about Czech lands. This appeasement,
we now know, appeased Hitler for about an hour. This
is what happens when you confuse Chinese food with
diplomacy.

Hitler then decided he wanted the rest of the country,
too. No problem, now that England and France had given
him the green light, he just took the entire region.

Meanwhile, back in Slovakia, the Slovak Peoples Party,
with Nazi backing, set up a puppet government under a
Catholic priest, Tiso. Even today, Slovaks can't decide if
Tiso was a good guy or a bad guy. His image is undergoing
rehabilitation (revised positively), since Slovakia is a little
short of heroes. The Democrats are doing the same thing
with Bill Clinton, for the same reason.

The Slovaks do celebrate this period of independence, since they had been under Hungarian, Austrian, or Czech control for about a million years prior to this. Things steadily got worse for everyone, except some communists, until finally the Slovaks were desperate enough to try something, anything.

Hoping that the Russians would come to their aid, being fellow Slavs, they launched the Slovak National Uprising in the mountains of central Slovakia. This uprising failed immediately when the Russians failed to appear. This non-event remains an icon of nationalist feeling to this day. It is the only show of resistance the Slovaks have put up in the face of an invading army, in about 2000 years.

Meanwhile, later that same day in another part of Europe, General Patton was in Pilsen in western Bohemia. On May 5th, the people of Prague decided to try their luck at enticing Patton to liberate Prague, so they sent a cute young girl with an invitation. No dice. The allies left Prague to the Russians. Oops.

Soon after the end of the war, the reprisals began, when the Sudenten Germans became the target. Putting them on the same rations that the Jews had been given early in the war, two and one half million Germans in the Czech and Slovak Republics were starved to death, murdered, kicked out, or they fled for their lives. All over Eastern Europe, ethnic cleansing was applied to eleven million Germans. And you thought the Serbs invented it.

Sometime later, when Vaclav Havel got out of jail and into the presidents office, he apologized to the German people for all that ethnic cleansing. Most Czechs thought he was being a wimp, and that Germans got what they deserved. The new regime tried to do the same thing to the Hungarians, but were less successful.

Things bubbled along for years with the usual five-year economic plans that never seemed to work, and show trials of traitors that always worked. It slowly kept getting worse until finally the young Slovak, Alexander Dubcek, somehow finagled his way to be the First Secretary in 1968. Dubcek wanted slow, cautious reform. However, the pent up energy exploded everywhere into what came to be called the "Prague Spring."

Now optimism was everywhere, thick in the air like birds in a Hitchcock movie, and the proposed action program called "socialism with a human face" appeared. As the summer rolled along, so did the momentum, until it scared the kaka out of the leaders of other Warsaw Pact countries. Along with the summer, the Soviets rolled the tanks, and the Prague Spring died. A victim of exposure to the harsh realities of winter in a Prague occupied by legions of foreign troops.

Business continued as usual until the events of our time. The fall of the wall in 1989 finally gave people everywhere the courage to act on their own behalf. As people in America rediscover every day, while democracy brings problems, it is worth it.

Hold it. Time out. Stop. With all of the problems, crises, lawyers, disasters, soap operas, politicians, tragedies and minor irritations of life in America we need to say a little prayer (Supreme Court willing) of THANKS, right now. "Democracy is the worst form of government," Churchill was wont to say, "except all those other forms that have been tried from time to time."

Possibly the most critical problem will turn out to be that the Czech and Slovak people let the leaders decide to split the country in two, without a vote or referendum. The most persuasive speaker in Slovak politics, a snake oil salesman named Mecier, came up with an idea. Think Jesse Jackson with real power.

I'm tired of being a third rate politician, in a third rate part of Czechoslovakia, in a third rate part of the world, Mecier mused, *I wanna be the head of my own country, like a king, maybe. Yeah, that's it, I wanna be a king. There must still be a crown around here somewhere.*

One freezing day in November 1992, with sleet falling outside the window of his third rate palace, Mecier called Playwright President Havel of Czechoslovakia, up on his cell phone:

"Hey, Vaclav buddy," he said, "how about we rename our country 'Slovakoczechia' or something like that? And I'll be the president."

"No way," Havel responded, "I'm the playwright president, you're just desperate to be a despot."

"Hey, you got your own country," Mecier said, "I want my own country, too."

"Too bad," Havel said, "we can only have one president. I'm it, and you're not."

"Yeah, well," said Mecier, "in that case, I quit. I'm putting up a fence at the border, and you can't come down and waterski in the Danube anymore, so there." This is the same tactic that worked when Slovenia and Croatia quit Yugoslavia, if you don't count the civil war and ethnic cleansing when the other republics tried to leave.

"I'm not renaming Czechoslovakia," said Havel, "and I don't feel like a civil war either, so you got yourself a country." This just proves the old adage, *be careful what you wish for, you might get it.*

So Mecier got to be the king of his own little country. Slovakia has almost no industry (except the arms and munitions factories the communists put here), almost no foreign investment (except the odd tourist), and almost no prospects for any almost anytime soon.

They do have a national capital. Like a banana republic where the national anthem is *yes, we have no bananas.* Most

Slovakia is dog country, big time. Oh yeah,
once in a while you see a girl, too.

people I spoke with have mixed feelings about the divorce,
like children from a broken home. Older people savor
a taste of independence before they die. Young people,
however, see the Czech economy go whizzing past, and
fear they are road kill on the highway to the west.

STAR TRACK

A bright young woman, who works as an administrative
assistant at Slovak U in my department, is a tennis maniac
just like me. We play after work every chance we get, but
it occurs to us that we could play a lot more if we played
on the weekends.

The problem is that Patricia is from a small town
about fifty kilometers east of Bratislava. Even though she
has a room here in town during the week, she goes home
every weekend to see her friends and to help her parents
around the panelak. Finally, one of us is clever enough
(O.K., O.K. it was Patricia) to suggest that I come out to

her town to play on the weekends, since the train takes only about 35 minutes and costs about 35 cents.

One fine Saturday morning in May finds me on the train to Galanta. First, we pass through the standard industrial area that is the same one that surrounds the train station in every city.

Then we pass through the garden belt. This is the cluster of weekend gardens that surrounds every eastern European city. The place where weary communists escape the pressures of not thinking during the workweek. As we whiz through the fertile fields of the Danube River basin, it seems I have transported back in time to, say, the 1950's in the USA.

The fields are the same green as the fields in Nebraska. The sky is the same blue as the sky in Missouri. The plowed furrows are as straight and true as the furrows in Kansas. John Doe on his John Deere couldn't plow any better. The dirt is the same rich black dirt in Iowa. The weeds never stop growing just like in gardens all over America. The corn is as high as an elephant's eye.

That's it, I am in Iowa, and I know it is the 1950's because the tractors and the cars I see look like the ones in the Midwest in the 1950's. Well, almost like them. I see a car that could be a 1953 Plymouth, except that the headlights look as if they are from a 1955 Ford. I see a guy driving a tractor that reminds me of a tractor that my grandfather had on his farm up in northern Idaho. No wait, its not a Massy-Ferguson, it's a Massive-Fugitive. What is that license plate, some kind of new Canadian plate I've never seen?

See those telephone poles running alongside the track? They could be from Ohio, but I have never seen telephone poles with cross bars like that. And what about those signs? And those railroad crossing bars? Almost exactly like Tennessee, but not quite.

Remember that episode of Star Trek where Kirk and Spock found themselves stranded on a planet that was almost exactly like earth, circa 1940? As they walk around, they see guys wearing Nazi uniforms and jackboots. They almost believe they have somehow traveled back in time, to an earth that existed years before. Wait, something is not quite right, but Kirk and Spock can't quite put their finger on it. Then it dawns on them, everything is as earth would have been, if Germany had won World War II. The Nazis are in control of everything, and there is a totalitarian government.

This sounds like a harmless fantasy on my part. The scary part is when I read in the paper here that the best-selling novels in Japan concern revisionist history. These tell a nice little story about the world after World War II, how the world is now that the Japanese won the war.

The Germans are making speeches and writing articles about how they were victims in the Second World War. Excuse me, isn't this where we came in? The biggest German political party has a new slogan, a "self-confident country full of self-confident people."

That's what the world needs, an arrogant nation full of arrogant people, who have a history of insisting that everyone in the world be just like them, or else. This would be a real do-or-die situation. The sociologists are already talking about how the 20th century is the "century of war," how we have had more wars, and killed more people than the law allows. It could get worse.

To Market To Market

Saturday morning. To a fellow professor named Kate and me, this means the outdoor flea market at Nivy. This is not just another flea market, however, here you can get anything you want, just like Alice's Restaurant. From fresh fruits and vegetables, to radishes to bananas, from lettuce to oranges, to tomatoes to pineapple. There are stands with loaves of bread stacked sky high, stands with high piles of Asian made toys, stands with huge heaps of Chinese made clothes. There are blue jeans made all over the world hanging from every tree limb and rafter.

The aisles are only about one meter wide, but this doesn't stop extended families of twenty or thirty people from cruising side-by-side-by-side, stopping at each stand to inspect the goods, and chatter excitedly about each treasure. This is the place where the poor sell junk to the even poorer. Where successful businessmen have a six foot wooden stand with a roof, and the newest entrepreneur wannabes have an apple box for their store.

Everything is splashed with a name brand. The running shoes shout that they are by "Niki," the jeans scream that they come from "Levys;" the toys claim to be from "Metal." The watches howl "Seico," the T-shirts shriek "Adidis," and the baseball caps cry "Chicago Bolls." You can outfit yourself from head to toe with ersatz threads.

I can't figure out if the guys who make this stuff are trying to avoid a lawsuit, or just don't have a spell checker on their computer. Nothing is wrapped, not even the freshly killed and freshly cleaned chickens. There is no guarantee that the merchandise will work, there is no guarantee that the vendor will be here an hour from now, much less next week.

It is like a county fair, a traveling carnival, and a flea market at the abandoned drive-in in small town America, all rolled into one. There are brightly colored foods. There are gaily-colored clothes. There are Asians selling and Slovaks buying. There are Romanies selling and everyone buying. There are kids running and dogs barking. There are grandmas carrying babies and kids showing grandpas around. There are farmers selling and tourists buying. It is life in Eastern Europe. It is life everywhere.

PICNIC TIME

At lunchtime, we decide to get some picnic goodies at the local potraviny and sit in the garden of the local castle. It is a beautiful, warm, spring day and we are enjoying enjoying watching the ducks swim around in the wading pool out in the middle of the castle grounds.

Wait a minute, that's not a duck, that's some kind of black bird swimming around the pond. Wait a minute, it's not swimming well. Wait a minute, it can't swim at all, and it's drowning. While we are trying to figure out what to do, one of the young men on the bench next to us dashes down to the pool, jumps in, grabs the blackbird, and carries it back to dry ground. As the blackbird shakes itself off, and our hero walks back to his bench drying himself off, the rest of us give them both a standing ovation.

On the bus home from the market, the bus is crowded, as usual. Standing room only, and not much of that. Nothing unusual in this, but this trip is clear across town. Finally, we make the turn for home, and Kate and I get ready to fight our way to the door.

Suddenly, about two hundred meters from the bus stop, the bus stops. This is not unusual either; many times the bus must stop for another bus, a car, a kid, or a dog. But this time, the doors open and everyone bails out. This is unusual. Not a word is said, not a look is exchanged, but since everyone is stampeding, we get off too, the well documented lemming effect.

After we are standing on the ground, we look around to see what is going on. The bus has a flat tire. O.K. so the bus has a flat tire, what is so unusual about that? Nothing unusual, absolutely nothing. Buses here have flats on a schedule. What we can't figure out is, how did they know? How did the other people on the bus know about the flat? We were on the bus, there were no announcements, everybody just decided to bail at the same instant.

We try to analyze the situation. "Did you hear the one about the thermos bottle?" I ask Kate.

"No," is her response.

"A doctor and an engineer are discussing what they consider to be the most significant technological advances of our time," I said, "the doctor claims that medicine is the most amazing thing, but the engineer said it's nuclear power. They argue back and forth, until the janitor mopping the floor interrupts them. 'No,' the janitor said, 'it isn't either of those; the most amazing thing today is the thermos bottle.' 'What are you talking about?' they chime in unison. 'Well,' the janitor slowly drawls, 'if you put something hot in the thermos, it stay hot, and if you put something cold in, it stays cold. How does it know?'" Kate doesn't crack a smile.

"Got any other bright ideas?" she said.

"Nope, you?" I said. Silence. We think harder. We rack our brains, whatever that means.

"I have a theory," Kate finally announces.

"I don't have a clue," I admit, "what's your theory?"

"Collective mind," she said.

"Huh?" I retort brilliantly.

"The Slovaks have a collective mind, like the Borg on Star Trek," Kate explains, "when one knows something, they all know something."

I should explain here that Kate is younger than I am. I only watched the original Star Trek, and don't know about the Borg.

"That's ridiculous," I said.

"Got a better theory?" Kate presses her advantage.

"Not really," I sigh.

"That's it then," Kate finishes, "case closed."

12

Big Finish

"The wise are instructed by reason,
average minds by experience,
the stupid by necessity,
and the brute by instinct."

\- Marcus Tullius Cicero

It's good that some people here speak a little English, and most people speak a little German. Whenever I try to actually use the few Slovak words I have managed to learn, the person I am speaking with gets that "deer in the headlights" look. Even when I am going for a simple word, like the Slovak word for cold, "studene."

Example: I go into a restaurant to get a Coca Cola™, which should be a piece of cake. Everyone in the world understands Coke. Of course, half of the time they give you Pepsi Cola™. The various colas are interchangeable here, like presidential candidates in America. I order: "Coca Cola, pazalsta." Pazalsta means 'please'. The answer: "ano" means "good" but I take it as O.K.

Then I say "studene?" I don't want JUST a Coca Cola, I want a COLD Coca Cola, which is a much more difficult proposition here in Eastern Europe. Now the trouble starts. I repeat the word, I pronounce it different ways, I try pantomime, I sing a chorus of "I'd like to buy the world a Coke." Nothing, nada, zipski.

Sometimes I try German, sometimes a bilingual Good Samaritan will come to my aid, and sometimes I give up and accept a room temperature cola. Room temperature drinks are the norm here, in any case. Others have the same trouble here, more so than in other countries.

While I am figuring out how to get a cold Coke, I think of the Gary Larson cartoon about being constitutionally unable to understand a different language.

Cartoon caption: What we say to dogs: "Okay Ginger! I've had it! You stay out of the garbage! Understand Ginger? Stay out of the garbage, or else!"

What dogs hear: "Blah, blah, ginger, blah, blah, blah, blah, blah, blah, blah, blah, ginger, blah, blah, blah, blah."

I'm not comparing Slovaks to dogs. The average Slovak understands a lot more English than I understand Slovak. I am the dog in this cartoon.

Nevertheless, I have developed a theory. My theory is that in America we are used to hearing people from every nationality around the world butcher words in English. We have heard British accents, French accents, Texas accents, Swedish accents, Germans accents, Pakistani accents, Boston accents, and a hundred others.

When we hear someone with a new accent trying to pronounce the word "cold" we have a bunch of patterns in our data bank to compare it to. Here in Slovakia, people have no experience listening to foreigners mangle their language. So when they hear someone who is not a native Slovak speaker try to say "studene," they can't comprehend our babbling. Nah, I guess it's just me.

This is not a Slovakian leaning tower of Pisa.
The communist idea of religion
was slightly askew.

Another thing that exasperates Americans, especially American women, is the name game. With Slavic languages, a women's name always ends in "ova," like the tennis players Hana Mandlikova and Martina Navratilova.

People here add an "ova" to every woman's name, no matter what. They also insist on Eastern Europeanizing names. When someone from here moves to America, sometimes they change their name for whatever reason, but we don't insist that they do. Here, Kate Zurack instantly becomes Katja Zurackova, whether or not she wants to change her name. Don't ask. I don't know.

You know how delivery services work in the U.S., right? If something small needs to be delivered, a guy jumps on his bike (O.K., O.K. I know it might well be a girl, humor me) and flies through traffic. A bigger package and it is the same guy in a baby pickup flying through traffic.

Here in Slovakia, we do things a little bit differently. First, we are on Central European Time and nobody flies anywhere. If you send a small package, some guy strolls through Old Town with it, stopping for a glass of wine at a sidewalk café on the square. Second, if it is a bigger package, it's the same guy pushing a baby buggy with the package inside. You gotta love a country that doesn't allow cars in Old Town.

Growing Up Is Hard To Do

Once, taking a break from serious course work, I ask my students what they want to be when they grow up, I mean when they get out of school. Each thought for a time, got a real serious look on their face, and announced solemnly that they would like to work for a bank. I guess this makes sense, banks are where the money is, banks have all the nice new buildings, and it doesn't seem like the work is too hard. In fact, it seems hardly like work at all. You don't need a degree or qualifications. Perfect.

This gets me to thinking about what the world would be like if everyone worked for a bank. I mean if everyone made money just using money, and not doing anything useful, like Donald Trump. I call the Donald on his cell phone to ask him if he is still rich. His ex-wife is Czech, and is the one who started calling him "the Donald" due to grammar differences between English and Czech. I heard he just trademarked the phrase.

"So, Donny," I start out, "how's it hanging?"

"I'm rich," he said, "you can't call me Donny."

"O.K., O.K.," I said, "How rich are you?"

"I'm so rich, I could buy Eastern Europe with my lunch money," he said.

"So they say," I said, "how did you make all of that money?"

"I'm smart," Trump said.

"No, really," I said, "How did you get so much money?"

"I make deals," Trump said, "did you read my book?"

"Uh, sorry, not yet," I said, "exactly how do you make a deal?"

"Well, just between you and me," Trump whispers, "I don't know. My lawyers have me sign some papers, and then my accountants tell me that I made a bunch of money. Of course lately, they tell me I lost a bunch of money."

"Let me get this straight. You mean you don't know how to make a deal yourself?" I said.

"No way," finished the Donald, "I gave that up after Ivana cleaned me out in the divorce."

Taxi Driver

Last summer, when I told my mom that I was going to be teaching in Eastern Europe, she didn't ask what I would be teaching or how much money I would make. She didn't even ask if it was a war zone.

The Carlton Hotel, after reconstruction.
And new light bulbs.

All year she has been impatiently waiting to see Vienna. Now she is here, and we are going to Vienna tomorrow. Today we are taking one of the new EC trains up to Brno in the Czech Republic, as a tune-up.

When we arrive in Brno, we wander around the local Stare Mesto for a while, getting the lay of the land. Deciding it is time to play real tourist, we get out the guidebook and start looking for the closest museum.

Reading a guidebook qualifies you as a target in Eastern Europe, and immediately a pleasant looking guy comes up and asks in German if he can help. Since we don't need any help, and since we don't know what kind of help he has in mind, we decline, in English. He immediately switches gears and repeats his offer in perfect English. Again we decline, this time in German, so he reluctantly goes on his way, a puzzled look on his pleasant face.

The first museum on the list is right across the street from where we are standing, so we cross over and go in followed by three middle-aged, overweight women. At a table just inside the door sits an elderly man, the gatekeeper. He explains, in Czech, to all five of us that most of the museum is closed, but we can see a display of Bonsai trees imported from Japan for only ten crowns (about forty cents). In spite of this tempting offer, we all decline, not wanting to dilute our communist touristing with Asian stuff.

In unison, we turn to leave. As we get to the door, the first heavyweight woman steps adroitly between my mom, who is in the lead of our parade, and me. It is as if she momentarily morphs into a ballet dancer from the Bolshoi Ballet in Moscow. My mom goes out the door, followed by one extra large woman, who doesn't quite make it.

In the doorway, her sandal comes off of her foot, and she bends over to put it back on. I am stuck between her overly generous derriere, and two equally corpulent women bringing up the rear, so to speak.

As the over-sized woman in the doorway struggles fruitlessly to get her sandal on, the two women behind me are pushing me inexorably forward, like lava going downhill. They seem surprisingly eager to get outside, making me the filling in an unwilling sandwich.

As I am about to say something rude, I feel a hand go in the outside pocket of my camera bag, which is hanging from a strap on my shoulder. I grab the bag and whirl around to face my plump pickpockets.

Wait a minute, I think, *these women look like, well, like Romanies. Yeah, they are Romanies.* While this realization registers on my face, the three nymphs nimbly skip out the door and disappear into the crowd. I check the bag, but there had been nothing in the outside pocket, and the other pockets were still securely zipped shut. I was aware of Romanies, I thought I was ready for Romanies, and they had still gotten a hand in my bag.

The performance was smooth and slick, and they were a well-rehearsed and polished team. If you saw this magic act on the stage, you would have applauded enthusiastically. Siegfried and Roy would have some competition. We were lucky there was nothing in that pocket.

As if to prove we were lucky, the next day we ran into a friend of mine back in Bratislava who had almost the same experience, except she lost her wallet with money, credit cards, and passport to the same bravura performance.

Meanwhile, we go into a shop to buy some postcards to prove that we have really been in Brno. The thin, middle-aged, attractive woman running the shop warns us: "be careful with your bag, Romanies are in town." We thank her and admit we have already been introduced. As we walk around town that afternoon, we suddenly see Romanies everywhere, standing in small groups, giving each passerby the eye.

We have another encounter with a larger, younger, slimmer band that get between us on some stairs. By now I am clutching my bag with both hands like Gale Sayers holding onto the football on the one-yard line, so they concentrate on my mom.

When they discover she isn't carrying a purse anymore (her stuff is in my bag as a precaution) they finally decide to leave us alone, and we aren't approached the rest of the day. It almost seems as if they mark you, somehow, when they decide they aren't going to score, so other Romany bands don't waste their time on you. Don't ask. I don't know.

Taxi Dancer

Arriving back in Bratislava past the normal bus time, we decide to take a taxi out to the quaint little village of Devin instead of waiting for the night buses to start. Approaching the taxi stand, we stop at the first cab in line and inquire how much he would charge for the trip. Using some Slovak, some German, and some English, we first establish that we want to go to the Village Devin, and not the upscale Hotel Devin right around the corner.

"How much for a taxi to the quaint little village of Devin?" I ask.

"One thousand, six hundred crowns" (about $54), he said.

"Do you mean one hundred sixty crowns?" I ask after we all have a good laugh at this joke.

"Oh no," he replies earnestly, "two zeros."

Since I know this trip would run a Slovak about one hundred crowns, tops, I figure we have a big target painted on our foreheads, again. We go on down to the cab at the end of the line and try again.

"How much for the taxi to the quaint little village of Devin?" I ask.

"Two hundred and fifty crowns, more or less," is the answer.

"I would like to know exactly,'" I reply. This guy somehow knows we aren't newbies, but I don't want a surprise.

"I can't say, exactly," he said, "I have a meter and I must charge whatever the meter says. It could be more."

Having played this game before, and lost, we go around the corner to the cabs in front of the recently reconstructed Carlton Hotel.

"How much for the taxi to the quaint little village of Devin?" I ask.

"No problem, do you want a price to the center of Devin," the driver said, "or directly to your house?"

Of course he said this half in Slovak and half in German and half in sign language, but you get the idea.

It's finally final exam time, class.
Is this a communist ski jump into the trees,
or are they building a highway to the west?

My cottage is close enough to the center of the three street village, so he quotes a price of one hundred fifty crowns (less than $5 bucks). Deal.

Arriving in the quaint little village of Devin, we find Burciak waiting, meowing for food. Putting out her dish, I make a mental note to leave money with the village people, to buy cat food after I leave. They agree, but they just say "nie" to kitty litter.

SCHOOLS OUT

My classes are over. I had told my students they would be making an oral presentation of their final paper to the rest of the department. The day before the big day, a small delegation of students show up at my office.

"We have a beeg problem," the spokesperson begins.

"What is that?" I venture.

"No one in the class is coming to do the presentation tomorrow," she said.

"What do you mean no one?" I said.

"I mean not a single person is coming to class tomorrow," she finishes.

"Not even you three guys?" I wonder.

"Not even us," she agrees happily.

"What's going on?" I ask, "Is it some kind of a Eastern European holiday? Maybe it's Trotsky's birthday, or the anniversary of the Russian invention of the tractor?"

"No holiday," she cheerfully admits, "just no one is coming to class anymore."

"O.K., I'll bite," I sigh, "what is really going on?"

"We decided," she said firmly, "that classes are over and we aren't going to do the presentation."

"You decided?" I said, "I thought that sort of thing is my decision?"

"Well, we talked it over and made a collective decision," she said a little proudly, "we decided no one is coming to the presentations." She was right. Class was over. I just didn't know it and I never saw my students again. Don't ask. I just don't know.

BIG FINISH

What this story needs is a big finish: a terrorist, a bomb, a crash, a coup. Too bad I don't have one. What I do have is a lasting image of life in Eastern Europe.

The last morning, I decide to take a final stroll through the cobblestone streets of stare mesto. Walking through the square, I stop to watch a young couple play fetch with their German Shepard. It is a fitting last scene, since Slovakia is dog country, big time.

Wait a minute, something is wrong here. Let's see, the girl throws the ball, and the dog runs after it. Instead of the dog picking up the ball, the man picks up the ball and throws it back. The dog chases the ball again, but the girl has to go over and pick it up and throw it back. The dog chases the ball again, like dogs the world over.

When I get close enough to see what is going on, I see that the dog is wearing the mandatory muzzle, and he can't pick up the ball.

The dog wants to play fetch, the people want to play fetch, but they have a beeg problem. The former Soviet Bloc dog has been wearing the muzzle his entire life, and his father wore one before him. He doesn't really mind wearing it, and he's probably just now figuring out that dogs in other countries don't have to wear a muzzle. Try it sometime, it does make life different if you wear a muzzle.

Now is the end of the year of living not so dangerously. It is time to go home.

Hasta La Vista, Communista!

About Me

I should have been born in Texas, my parents were living there at the time. However, they were on the road that day, and I was born in New Mexico. We moved to Idaho before I was six months old, and I have since lived and traveled all over the USA. Except the Northeast, of course. I attended eight schools in twelve years, then began college in Honolulu, and finished in Miami. I love the weather in California, the rocks in Utah, the horses in Texas, the ocean in Florida, and golf courses everywhere. Except the Northeast, of course.

I am married, with children. My wife, Larysa, is from Ukraine. Our son Will was born in Florida, and our daughter Grace in North Carolina. On the road, our faithful companion Panda, an Australian Shepard, accompanies us.

I have taught policy analysis, urban planning and public management in universities and graduate schools in Florida, California, Slovakia, and Kazakhstan. I am currently teaching information systems at a college in North Carolina, and am working on another book. This one will be serious, of course.

LaVergne, TN USA
16 December 2010
209086LV00003B/8/A